In the Shadow of the Crane

A Life in Short Stories
and Tall Tales

John Keeman

RINGWOOD PUBLISHING
GLASGOW

First published in Great Britain in 2020
by
Ringwood Publishing, Glasgow.
www.ringwoodpublishing.com
mail@ringwoodpublishing.com

ISBN 978-1-901514-82-7

British Library Cataloguing-in-Publication Data
A catalogue record for this book is available from the
British Library

Printed and bound in the UK
by
Lonsdale Direct Solutions

Dedication

I dedicate these writings to my friend of many years George Miller. Sadly George died in July this year.

The writer Terry Prachett said: 'No one is actually dead until the ripples they cause in the world die away.'

In that case my friend George will be around for a very long time.

Introduction

City I am True son of thyne
Ne'er dwelt I where great mornings shine
Around the bleating pens
Ne'er by the rivulets I strayed
 And ne'er upon my childhood weighed
The silence of the glens
Instead of shores where ocean beats
I hear the ebb and flow of streets
A sacredness of life and death
Dwells in thy noise and Smokey breath

Alexander Smith 1829-1867

It took me a long time to decide to write this autobiography. On the one hand, I thought such writings were restricted to the rich and famous, who have often used the genre to excuse some outrageous behaviour or to apologise for it. On the other hand, there is no reason why an ordinary guy with no claim to fame, nor a fleeting romance with it, should not write about his life. My Warhol moment came in 1959 when I drove a 1949 Jaguar car from inside a car showroom, through a plate glass window out into the street and got my picture in the *Daily Express* the following day. No criminal charges were brought as the police deemed the incident a 'private accident'. I did get some letters from teenage girls and I decided to visit the one who lived nearest. She lived in the quaint little village of Drumchapel. When I knocked on her door, she opened it, but before anything could be said, her father appeared, chased her inside and threatened to beat me up. Fame obviously was not for me I decided and made my way home. Saddened but still having my own teeth.

In our present-day society I would probably be invited to appear on television and explain what happened *ad nauseum*. But life wasn't like that back in the 1950s. There was a clear line drawn between celebrities and nonentities, but that line has become increasingly blurred over the years. Having flicked through some tomes written by so-called celebrities, I figured my life, and that of any other human being, is just as important to record as theirs. This book records my life and the times I lived in, from the poverty and depression of the 1940s and 50s, through to the early decades of the new millennium.

Chapter One

Growing up in Anderston

I was the first child of Jean and John Keeman, born in my great aunt Margaret's house in Finnieston Street under the crane that bore the street's name. My mother, a small woman with a glass eye and a ferocious temper, was an unemployed tearoom waitress, and my dad worked at a railway yard in the Gallowgate.

In June 1944 the D-Day Landings signalled the beginning of the end of the Second World War. As I grew up, I was surrounded by the paraphernalia of war: ration books, ID Cards, army belts, boots, caps, and greatcoats with enormous brass buttons. The streets were full of uniformed men and limbless ex-servicemen sang round the back courts or sold matches on street corners.

That same year a Danish scientist, Niels Bohr, wrote to Winston Churchill and Theodore Roosevelt stating: 'A weapon of unparalleled power is being created. Unless some international agreement about the control or use of the new active materials can be obtained, any temporary advantage, however great, may be outweighed by the perpetual menace to human society.'

The following year America dropped two atomic bombs on Japan, finally bringing the war in the Pacific to an end and heralding the start of the atomic age into which I was born.

The family home was a single-end at 44 Guest Street in Anderston, but I have no memory of the inside of this particular house. The first house I can remember living in was another single-end at 25 Oak Street. That house was on the third floor of a tenement and I remember it had a fireplace, a cavity bed, a sink, a cupboard and little else. It was lit by a gas mantle above the fireplace and the toilet was on the landing downstairs. The Single End dwellings were single rooms with no bath or toilet. They were designed for two adults and, at the most, two children under twelve. In reality, much larger families occupied these hovels. Ours was a depressing house, in a depressing area, in a depressing society.

It was from here that I journeyed on a grey Monday morning in 1949 to begin my schooling at the age of five. Less than ten minutes later I entered through the enormous doors of Finnieston Primary School. I remember crying when my mother left me with a grey-haired old woman. I hated school on that first day and the feeling stayed with me for the next ten years. At every opportunity I feigned illness, lied, or found some other excuse to avoid going. Excuses weren't difficult to find as I seemed to catch every sickness that was going: measles, mumps, bronchitis, chicken pox, abscesses, toothache and boils, to mention a few.

The streets and backcourts were the playgrounds for kids growing up in Anderston in the 1940s and 50s. With real toys in short supply, children improvised. A piece of wood and a bean tin made an excellent tomahawk. A bread board from the local bakery was a good start to making a bogey, and ball bearings for the wheels could be had from the workers in the local engineering factory in Lancefield Street. With a couple of pieces of wood for axles and string for the steering, you could knock a bogey together in a short time.

Pavement stanks provided a source of fun trying to fish out money dropped by drunks. A magnet, with some grease spread on the bottom, attached to a piece of string made a fine rod for coins.

Girls chalked the pavements with peever beds and boys played football on any spare ground they could find. We played on a hill between Oak Street and Guest Street and the

2

cry went up by the winner after the toss: 'We'll kick up hill in the first half!' The same piece of land was used for sleds made of bread boards when it snowed and bonfires on the 5th November. On one such night a couple of my pals found some bullets in an old office next to the Hydepark Street stables and threw them in the fire. When they got very hot, they went off with a bang, but amazingly no one was hurt.

There was a plumbers' merchant, called R. M. Donald, on Oak Street with a lamppost right outside the door. On winter's nights we would chalk a dart board on the door and play darts under the light of the lamppost. The door was like a pin cushion but nobody ever complained.

Climbing on the top of midden roofs and dykes were other sources of amusement, albeit somewhat risky. Some of the latter were topped with half-round, reddish-brown tiles that were notoriously slippery in wet weather. On one occasion I ended up with one leg in a midden bin, and the other outside, resulting on a trip to Yorkhill Children's Hospital and an introduction to something called iodine. This made your skin go yellow and blue and nipped like hell - but it got me off school for a few days. I was later knocked over by a car in Stobcross Street, when I ran across the road without looking, resulting in another leg injury, iodine treatment and time off school.

My mother's attitude to education helped as she didn't really care whether I went to school or not. Being absent meant she could send me on errands to Lindsay's Dairy, a few doors down from the Post Office on Stobcross Street. I had an auntie, Cathy McLaughlan, who lived across the road from the dairy and my mother always told me not to go into the shop if she was there. I expect she didn't want her to know she was getting food on credit. Going to the dairy was usually an embarrassing experience as my mother rarely had the money to pay for the groceries and I had to ask for credit. Sometimes the man in the brown overalls would give me what my note asked for without any trouble, but on other occasions he would tell me my mother had to come herself. I suppose that was when she had exceeded her credit limit for the week.

My dad had the same casual approach to education, having left school himself at the age of twelve, and run away to sea. He could barely read or write but he had never been out of work, so he never thought there was any real value in going to school. However, whilst he was always in work, it was always a poorly-paid job and we struggled to make ends meet.

My younger sister Elizabeth, was born in July 1946. I have no recollection of that event, but I felt its impact when I was about eight years old and my mother decided there wasn't enough room in the single-end for the four of us and I was sent to live with my grandparents. They had a three-bedroom house in a tenement on the corner of Hydepark Street and Stobcross Street. The house was shared with my mother's three brothers: Billy, Tommy and James, and her younger sister, Margaret. I slept in my Uncle Tommy's room on a sort of make-shift bed with an army greatcoat for a blanket when it was cold in the winter. On many a winter's morning I awoke with the King's Own Scottish Borderers emblem firmly engraved into my temple, having fallen asleep with my head on one of the coat buttons.

Tommy didn't work. I believe he suffered from an illness contracted during his army service, but he was good with his hands. His room was more like a workshop than a bedroom and he spent a lot of his time repairing things like watches, clocks, radios, gramophones and other household items, and there was always a smell of machine oil, candle wax and wood shavings. As well as effecting repairs, Tommy also made wooden models and I remember I played a lot with a model of the British battleship 'HMS Hood.' Years later there were many arguments over the ownership of the model ship and it eventually disappeared out of the family.

Like his father and brothers, Tommy was fond of a drink and at night the house reeked of alcohol, tobacco and smoke from the coal fire. Many years later, when I was told by my doctor my chest problems were due to my smoking, I told him it was more likely caused by the damp living conditions in my grandmother's house and the fact that the six people living there with me all smoked like a chimney.

My uncles constantly argued and fought with each other and anyone else who wanted to 'have a go', and the police were frequent visitors to the Robertson household. My grandmother was a large woman crippled by rheumatoid arthritis and virtually housebound. The only times I recall her ever leaving the house were when local politicians drove her to the local school so she could cast her vote in a general or local election. Despite her health problems, she arose to put me out to school every morning, washing my face and neck with a cold flannel at the kitchen sink. The kitchen overlooked the roof of the Hamilton and Forbes Sawmill and, sometimes, when I was being washed for school, a rat would walk along the window ledge and jump on to the roof, disappearing into the mill. The house was over-run with mice but my grandmother assured me that this wasn't a bad thing as rats wouldn't enter a house where there were mice. The scientific basis of her pronouncement I have never explored, but it was somehow comforting.

Breakfast in those days usually consisted of porridge and black, sweet, stewed tea. As I remember, most other meals were just as unappetising. Cabbage and potatoes are the only vegetables I can recall having in those early years. These were generally accompanied by the ham from ham ribs or pig's feet, which were really revolting things to look at on a plate with the hairs still visible on the burned black skin. Eggs came in a tin, as did dried milk and orange juice.

School was tough and I ended up with more than my fair

share of black eyes, until I joined the boxing club. It wasn't long before I learned that I couldn't box eggs but I turned up every Wednesday evening and when word got around that I was a member, the bullies started looking elsewhere for their victims. I found out that some of the wee hard cases thought I was related to the champion boxer from Anderston, Peter Keenan, and would not risk a fight with me. Of course, I did nothing to put them wise as to their spelling mistake.

My mother came to my grandmother's every day but I didn't see my father often at that time. He worked long hours on the railway and rarely visited my grandmother's house. He was a non-drinker and never smoked and I don't think he got on with his in-laws. He was much older than my mother and was over forty when they married in 1943. My mother was 22.

My father went missing for quite a long time at one point and I only found out years later that he'd wound up in hospital for weeks, close to death. He was in a wooden hut in the railway yard having his break when a fellow workman used some petrol to get the fire started. The hut caught fire with my dad inside and he was badly burned. This explained the constant shortage of money and my mother's visits to the pawnshops in Elderslie Street and the City Pawnshop at the top of Washington Street at Anderston Cross. She pledged things like cutlery or bedclothes that she'd bought on credit from door-to-door salesmen, or from one of the credit warehouses in the city centre. One morning she took me with her to the pawnshop in Elderslie Street and on the way there we met her sister Margaret. I blurted out that we were going to pawn the clock and received a very thick and painful ear for providing this information.

When my dad finally recovered from his injuries, he was left with scars on his arms and upper body that you could still see quite clearly when he was in his eighties. Of course, his job had gone and he looked for work and ended up working with Easdales' scrap yard in Washington Street, before getting a job as a welder's helper with Barclay and Curle's shipyard on the Clyde, where he worked until he retired in the 1960s.

I continued to live with my grandparents while I was at Finnieston school, but in the summer the family would go on holiday together to Stevenston on the west coast of Ayrshire. Like many other working-class families who lived near the sea, the Grahams rented out a room in their family home to Glasgow people during the Glasgow Fair fortnight. Very few people went on holidays abroad as it was far too expensive for the average family. Years later, package holidays were developed, enabling some working-class families to visit Spain and other continental resorts.

Personally, I have never been out of the United Kingdom. I will not fly, which precludes foreign travel. My wife and children have taken many holidays abroad and from their experiences of airports, weather, delays, customs and so on. I wondered why they ever went back again. Most people say I have a fear of flying but I've always said it's a fear of crashing. I really do not know why I won't travel on an aircraft.

The first time I had the opportunity to do so was in my early twenties when my boss booked me on a flight to Birmingham to pick up a new truck. Immediately I responded by telling him to cancel and to book me on a sleeper train from Glasgow Central, which he did. I think the answer may lie in my childhood. I was quite a good reader, but I did not really read newspapers. On reflection, this was around the time the papers, and the *Pathe News* in the picture halls, were full of reports on aircraft crashes, in particular those involving the first commercial jet - the Comet. Three of these aircraft fell out of the sky in a single year due to metal fatigue. I suppose reading and watching reports on these crashes must have had some effect on a ten-year-old, but I suspect the National Health Service isn't about to book me an appointment with a psychologist to find out. Besides, I have fond memories of my holidays on the Ayrshire coast.

The Grahams had a large garden where they grew vegetables and kept hens and rabbits. The house was only a few minutes from the beach and when the weather was good, which wasn't often, I spent most of the day swimming in the ocean. My dad had taught me to swim when I was about six-years old by pushing me off the diving board in Cranstonhill Baths and diving in after me. It was a frightening introduction to the water and I wouldn't recommend it as a teaching method, but it worked for me, and I became a strong swimmer.

During school holidays if the weather was warm, I would go with some friends to the swimming baths. We would only wear swimming trunks and an old pair of sandshoes. We'd hide our shoes in the close next to the sweet shop across from the baths. Then we would sneak under the pay desk of the baths, run up the stairs and dive into the pool. The attendant was an old guy with a bad leg and by the time he got upstairs he had no idea who he was looking for. Moreover, he couldn't use the threat of throwing our clothes into the pool to get us to come out. I later swam in competitive galas for the Boys Brigade in public swimming pools around Glasgow. In one particular gala I was the final leg of the relay, but unfortunately, I dived in a split second before my teammate touched the bar; leading to the disqualification of the whole team. I won by half the length of the pool, but that made no difference to the rules-possessed-judges. Competitive swimming was not for me, I decided.

During one Glasgow Fair, I was sent to live with my Mother's eldest brother, John, at his home in Oakley, a village in Fife, whilst the rest of the family went to Stevenston as usual. Unlike his three brothers, who had been in the army, John was a merchant seaman. He was a strict disciplinarian and the holiday was not a pleasant experience. However, he did teach me to ride a bicycle during those two weeks by thumping me every time I fell off. When I returned to Glasgow, I begged my mother to buy me a bike, but my pleas fell on deaf ears. From time to time I managed to borrow a bicycle and I later discovered that a shop in St. Vincent Street rented bikes by the hour. When I managed to scrape together enough money, I would rent one for the day. I can still remember the freedom that something as simple as a bicycle brought. It enabled me to escape the noise and greyness of the city by cycling down to Balloch and sitting on the edge of Loch Lomond. Flat tyres were a nightmare. I'd push a punctured bike back to the shop, arriving after it was closed. The next day I had to haggle for keeping the bike beyond my contracted hours. The proprietor eventually taught me how to repair a puncture and these incidents occurred less frequently. I suspect he felt it was the cheaper option because I could never pay him the extra charges.

Whilst bicycles provide an escape in the physical sense, books were a form of psychological escape. Although I spent a lot of time absent from school, by the time I was eight I could read quite well and joined the Anderston Library in McIntyre Street. On cold winter evenings this was my haven, and I'd sit and read, well away from my mother's drunken brothers, soaking up the peace and quiet. The first book I borrowed on my library card was *Black Beauty* by Anne Sewell, the story about the adventures of a horse as it comes under the ownership of different characters. This was followed by Robert Louis Stevenson's *Treasure Island,* then Crompton's *Just William* books and later, Jules Verne. I felt rather proud when I got my first library ticket - a small piece of cardboard with a slot for a green ticket. When you borrowed a book, the librarian removed a small ticket from the slot on the book, placed it in the slot on the ticket and put the ticket in a large drawer under your name alphabetically. She then stamped the book with a return date and handed it over. It was all very official and you were fined if you returned the book late, around a penny a day. Over the years I must have paid a small fortune in library fines.

Generally speaking, it was not a good idea for a ten-year-old to read newspapers in the 1950s. They were full of stories about the new Hydrogen Bomb that was set to blow us all to kingdom come. Firstly, America had it and, a few months later, Russia. Then there were stories of nuclear submarines being developed and carrying enough nuclear missiles to blow up the world. It seemed like two world wars were not enough to satisfy the bloodlust. I was also terrified of people from Kenya, known as the Mau Mau, whose violent attacks with machetes featured regularly in the daily newspapers with as much bloodthirsty writing as the journalists could muster.

I remember my uncles, James and Billy, were set to be recalled to the Army when the Egyptian leader, Nasser, nationalised the Suez Canal. Violence, it seemed, was all around. There is a tendency for older people to wax lyrical about Glasgow in the old days, but the reality is that it was a violent city, but perhaps not quite as violent as John Stark, the main character in the book *No Mean City*, portrayed it. There were still gangs and there were the Glasgow hardmen, like my uncles. However, there was always music and, about two weeks before my tenth birthday, a group came along who changed music forever: Bill Haley and the Comets with the song, *Rock Around the Clock*.

The music charts of the early 1950s had people like Frankie Lane, Doris Day, Joe Stafford and Eddie Fisher. They were very talented singers, but did not perform the type of music that most young people wanted to hear. Bill Haley changed all that and soon after the words 'Rock and Roll' entered the language with names like Elvis, the Everly Brothers, Jerry Lee Lewis, Little Richard, Fats Domino, Cliff Richard, Marty Wilde, Billy Fury and a host of others. Some people declared it was violent music, but it was a violent world it was born into.

The cinema, or the pictures as Glaswegians say, was another form of escape and on Saturday mornings my dad would take me to the Gaiety Picture Hall in Argyle Street, near Anderston Cross, and fetch me after the matinee. They usually showed a cowboy picture with Roy Rogers or Hopalong Cassidy or Batman in black and white. The problem was that the storylines of Batman and Robin followed on until the next Saturday and if I couldn't get the money to go the next week I never found out how Batman was rescued from the burning building as he lay unconscious on the roof, which was beginning to cave in, or how he managed to escape unscathed from his Batmobile as it went over a cliff.

Money, or to be more precise the lack of it, was always an issue and it seemed, that apart from reading books, everything else came at a price. Although my uncles were fairly generous, particularly when they were drunk, I wanted a regular source of income. My first paid job was when I was nine or ten years old. I worked for Sanny Lang, a coalman who stayed up a close in Argyle Street, near the Buttery Restaurant, and stabled his horses in a lane off Hydepark Street. I got this job by hanging around the Minerva Street coal depot during the summer holidays and pestering the coalmen to let me look after the horses. I began to get work and my tasks were to fold the empty coal bags neatly on the cart after they were used and to feed and water the horses when the men were delivering the coal. I also had to make up the odd bag of coal by taking a few lumps from all the other bags, which the men sold for their beer money. At the end of each shift I helped remove the harness and wash down the horse at the stable in Heddle Place or the stables on Kent Road. Most of the customers got their coal on credit and on Friday evenings I would go round with the coalman to collect the week's money. I'd collect up one close while he did the next and so on. After a couple of weeks, I had my own little 'tick book' with the names of 'my customers' and how much they paid - or didn't, as the case sometimes was.

Those who paid every week usually gave me a tip, so between that and my 'wages' I usually had enough to hire a bike or go to the cinema, and I became a regular at the Gaiety, Kelvin, Tivoli, Rosevale and the Western picture halls. Of course, you could sometimes sneak into the cinema without paying but most of the time I tried this I was caught and dumped unceremoniously out on to the street. I had a number of similar jobs with other coal companies until the advent of motorised coal lorries saw them take over from the horses and I lost interest.

Horses figured heavily in Glasgow life in the early 1950s and my paternal grandfather, who was a carter with Black and White whisky in Washington Street, taught me how to drive the horse and cart. One day, on our way to the stables after work, we were heading up Washington Street toward Anderston Cross when he handed me the reins. Prince, a massive black and white Clydesdale, was ambling along quietly enough when we reached the top of the street. The traffic policeman on duty, as was his normal routine when he saw horses coming up the street, stopped the traffic coming through the Cross to give the horses an uninterrupted run over the brow of the hill. On that particular day he was wearing a white arm band and when he raised his arm, it spooked Prince who took off like a bat out of hell. He charged through the cross and headed west up Argyle street with me screaming and pulling as hard as I could on the reins. My grandfather's reaction was to laugh and yell at me to hang on, shouting Prince would run out of steam at the top of the street. Sure enough, just outside St. Mark's Lancefield Church, across the road from the Salvation Army, he ground to a halt. My grandfather told me to go into the Prince of Wales pub and get the 'silly bastard' a pail of water, whilst he lit up a Woodbine.

The official reason given by my mother for stopping me

going out with my grandfather on his cart was that it was interfering with my school-work, which in truth she had never bothered about before. In reality, the two of them never really got on. He was a strange old man who refused to stay for long in a house and slept rough in the summer or in the stables in winter. He was rarely sober, even at work, and always had a Woodbine dangling from his mouth, but he lived until he was 98 years old. When he was in his eighties, he was taken into the Western Infirmary by the police who found him lying on a bench at Anderston Cross. My dad came over to my house around midnight and we went up to the hospital. After we explained who we were, a doctor came to see us.

'This is my dad, John Keeman. My name is John Keeman as well. I believe my grandfather, also John Keeman, was admitted a short while ago. Can you tell us what's wrong with him?' I asked.

'I certainly can. He's drunk!' the doctor said. 'He can stay overnight but I want him out of here first thing in the morning.'

I told the doctor I would come early in the morning to pick him up but when I got there about eight o'clock, he had already discharged himself.

In later years I traced my grandfather's army records and discovered he was quite a guy. He was born around 1885 and volunteered for the army during the First World War in 1915. After his training at Stirling Castle with the Argyll and Sutherland Highlanders, he was transferred to the newly formed 8th Battalion Machine Gun Corps. On the 25th of April 1916 his Battalion was part of the British Expeditionary Force posted to France in 1916 and he was involved in a number of battles over the next two years during which he drove a team of horses delivering men and ammunitions to the Front and acting as ambulances on their return. His military records reveal that he remained in France until 27th of January 1919 and during his time there his wife and two daughters died from a lung disorder at home in Glasgow. When he returned to Britain he went back to his job as a carter and never remarried. He was quite a dour man, always ready for a fight, but when I think of what he must have went through during the war I can't blame him. His army records also show that whilst he fought in a number of battles against the Germans, he also had a running battle with his superior officers and was court martialled six times. He did some short spells in military prisons but one punishment I found to be particularly nasty was *Field Punishment Number 1*. This involved manacling the offender hand and foot and chaining him to a cannon, wagon or other fixed object for a maximum of two hours for each day of sentence. It was a punishment that could only be applied whilst a soldier was on active service overseas. In many instances, offenders were chained to an object within reach of enemy shellfire. Despite his railing against authority he managed to get two medals: The Victory Medal 1914-1919 and the British Medal WW1. Nice one Britain. In civilian life he returned to his job as a carter with the Black and White Whisky Bond and his later years were spent in Foresthall Hospital or, as it was known locally the 'poor's house', where he died around 1981.

Sometime before 1954 my mother's sister Margaret married a policeman. The police were frequent visitors to the Robertson household and, in a twist of irony, my Aunt Margaret ended up marrying one. His name was George and they moved into a nice flat up a tiled close in Kildonan Drive. However, this move toward becoming middle class did not go down well with the rest of her family. Moreover, she had brought a polis, of all people, into the family, which was the equivalent of marrying a psychopathic serial killer in the eyes of her brothers. George had spent most of his working life directing traffic at the junction of West Nile Street and West George Street, so the opportunities for corrupt practices were few and far between but nevertheless, that didn't stop the rumours that emanated from Margaret's disgruntled relatives.

One day I went to visit my aunt and discovered the house had wall-to-wall carpets, a radiogram, a three-piece suite, an electric fire, a living room, two bedrooms, a kitchen and an inside toilet. It was spotlessly clean. Every other house I'd visited in Anderston had wax cloth on the floors and smelled of smoke from the fireplace or cat's urine from the coal bunker. George was considerably older than Margaret and within a year or so of the marriage she gave birth to twin girls. I only ever met them once or twice when they visited my grandmother's house in Hydepark Street. Soon after one visit, George retired from the police and moved his family to Blackford in Perthshire. I never saw any of them again.

When my aunt moved out of Hydepark Street I was given her room. It was very small but it had a real bed. My uncle Tommy gave me an old radio he'd managed to get working and it opened up a whole new world. It introduced me to the world of drama, music, news and comedy through the BBC's Light Programme, Third Programme and the Home Service. Presently known as Radios Two, Three and Four respectively. Over fifty years later I still believe I learned more about the world through this media than I ever did in ten years of schooling. Of course, school had taught me how to read and write and do basic arithmetic but I wasn't the least bit interested in the lives of English kings, capital cities, the dates of famous battles or what colour litmus paper turned when it was dipped in an acid or alkali.

I certainly never understood the use of physical violence as a learning tool. Every time I got the belt it reinforced my view that school was simply a place where adults could assault children with impunity and I played truant even more. In later years my mother claimed she was fined by the School Board because I wasn't going to school but I never managed to verify this and I expect she wouldn't have paid the money anyway. In any event it didn't deter me from staying off school and when I wasn't working at the coal, I would hang around the dock sheds in the Broomielaw and help the carters load and unload their wagons which usually brought in a few pennies.

If there's one thing that stands out in my memories of my first ten years on earth, it's the poverty and strife that was all around. Most housing wasn't fit for a rat, there were few houses with indoor toilets, bathrooms were a luxury, and disease was prevalent all around. Yet people laid a great deal of importance on finding out whether you were a Catholic or a Protestant when they first met you. Every July the Protestants marched through the city in a show of violent discrimination against those of the Catholic faith and the Catholics retaliated by trying to break up the march or the more popular sport of having a kick at the big drum. The sad fact was that most of the people on both sides of the divide suffered the same poor housing conditions, lack of sanitation and threat of disease. They would have been far better off if they had protested against the politicians and City Fathers who allowed this state of affairs to continue whilst stuffing themselves at the City Chambers, or City Chancers, as it was known among Glaswegians. I remember the Orange Walk used to march down Hydepark Street below my Granny's window, heading for the Belfast Boat which sailed from the bottom of the street. It was certainly a colourful sight but every few yards yet another fight broke out and all the way down some people threw rubbish and other materials out their windows. I always regret that many of my family were bigots and involved themselves in this kind of behaviour. Of course, most activities a child could take part in when I was growing up had a religious base. School had its religious elements as did the Boys Brigade, the Scouts, Salvation Army, Band of Hope and all of their affiliates. Anyone would have thought that God featured as an important entity in people's lives but I can't remember any of these organisations protesting against the appalling conditions we were living in. It was all going to be better after you were dead was the war cry. I for one would have preferred my reward there and then rather than wait for heaven.

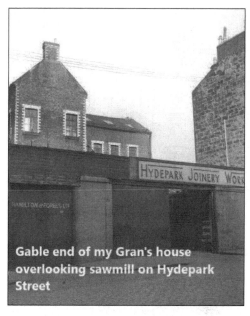

Grandmother's House, Hydepark Street

Chapter Two

School and Religion in the 1950s

In 1952 King George VI died and was succeeded by his daughter who became Queen Elizabeth II. Sometime in 1953 or 1954 she visited Glasgow and we were taken from school to Sauchiehall Street, given paper Union Jacks and told to wave them as she passed, on her way to the Kelvin Hall. I remember standing there sockless, in a pair of ragged short trousers, faded Sloppy Joe, snake belt and worn sandshoes, waving like an idiot at one of the richest women in the world. I'm sure she never noticed.

Around the same time, I joined the junior section of the Boy's Brigade and became a Lifeboy. This involved attending Bible classes and other activities during the week and church service on a Sunday. Near the end of the year I was getting washed at the sink in my grandmother's house in preparation for a Brigade Halloween party when she noticed the tell-tale signs of chicken pox on my back. I was immediately quarantined and sent to bed. It was so disappointing, but the next day an officer from the Brigade arrived at the door with apples, oranges, nuts and an armful of *Beano* and *Dandy* comics. I have never forgotten that kind gesture, but I grew tired of Bible classes and attending the church hall every week. Eventually, I quit the Brigade.

Not long after I left, I found myself at a church service one Sunday evening in the Salvation Army Hall in Argyle Street, across from the Prince of Wales pub. It was so different from all the other church services I had attended both with the Brigade and the school. I was mesmerised as I watched the

18

men and women playing in the band and found the noise of the brass instruments amazing. After the service I asked if I could join the band and learn to play an instrument and to my amazement, I was told I could. That night I became a member of the Salvation Army.

I attended band practice during the week and eventually learned to play the cornet. We practiced in a room in the cellar that you entered down a flight of stairs at the side of the stage. To me it was a magical place, with music stands on the floor, a piano, music books, brass instruments hanging from the walls and a roaring coal fire. I couldn't wait for the next practice night to come along.

Eventually I could play sufficiently well enough to become part of the band and on Sunday evenings I would take my place at the front of the hall with the band and blast out *Onward Christian Soldiers, Abide with Me, The Lord's My Shepherd* and other standard hymns. When Christmas came around, we played carols outside the local pubs and the men would come out and throw pennies into a hat. The bandleader was a very tall man with a pock marked face, who played the double bass. The instrument was almost as tall as I was and I wondered how he managed to lift it. Compared to the cornet the mouthpiece was enormous and when I finally got a note out of his bass he was overjoyed and so was I. He also taught me to play the trombone which was very different as it didn't have any keys and you sort of guessed where the note should be by moving the slider. I can't read a note of music anymore and I haven't blown into a mouthpiece for over sixty years, but I still have my original music books and a certificate from a Band Camp that I attended. This certifies that I passed in music theory and practice. I also still have the pledge I signed in 1955, vowing to abstain from all intoxicating liquor but that proved to be a pledge too far.

I had survived the first twelve years of my life but many kids around the area of Anderston did not. They succumbed to diphtheria, polio, rheumatic fever, bronchitis and other killers. In 1955 Winston Churchill stood down as Prime Minister, causing a General Election in May that year, which the Tories won by a landslide. My uncles, Billy and James, were back in uniform in Cyprus, where there was a rebellion against British rule. I was still in the uniform of the Sally Ann. In June 1956, I was selected to attend a Territorial Music School in Edinburgh. This was a Band Camp where we joined with other Salvation Army bands and were examined on musical practice and theory. The camp was set in grounds in a place called Middleton near Leith. I recall it was in an idyllic location with fields, woods and a lake. We were housed in long wooden buildings with dormitories and very basic amenities, but the food was good and we met fellow Salvationists from all around the world. The school lasted for two weeks and I made many new friends, but all our promises to keep in touch faded. We played outdoors on dry days and at the end of the school we received a certificate marking our performance. On one specific day I was late to take my seat and started playing a few bars behind everyone else. As far as I could make out when we finished, no one had noticed.

I retained my interest in the cinema, books, football and cycling but I could not find the motivation for schooling. My absence rate was high and as the class prepared to sit the 'qualifying exams' I was sure I would fail and remain at Finnieston until I was fifteen. If I passed, I had the opportunity to progress to Woodside Senior Secondary school and from there to university. I failed, of course, but things took an unusual twist when one of my teachers, a woman called Miss Hay, arranged to meet me along with my mother and father. I went over to my mother's house for the meeting at which Miss Hay outlined her view that she felt if I had tried harder and had fewer absences, I would have been capable of passing. She then proposed that if I was prepared to study hard over the next two weeks, I'd be given the opportunity to re-sit the exam. To this day I have no idea how she managed to arrange this, but I duly made the promise and spent almost every night after school in the Mitchell Library.

I was quite good with English and arithmetic but I struggled to get to grips with science, geography, mathematics and other subjects. Soon after I had sat the exam for a second time, I received a letter addressed to Master John Keeman. It advised that I was accepted for Woodside Senior Secondary School and would be expected to take my place there after the Easter holidays. One stumbling block was the requirement to wear a uniform that consisted of a maroon blazer and grey flannels, white shirt and maroon and grey striped tie and real shoes. Eventually, second hand equivalents were found and I started at Woodside aged twelve.

I was initially put into Class 1B where one of the subjects was French. Mister Burnett was the teacher and he started every class by having the children sing the National Anthem - *La Marseillaise.* To this day I often break into '*Allons enfants de la Patrie, Le jour de gloire est arrive*'. God knows why. One night many years later I was in the Pot Still with my mate, Ray. We met a couple of French guys, who spoke English very well, whereas our French was non-existent. After more than enough beers one of the French guys and me broke out into *La Marseillaise* and we sang it all the way through.

Mr Burnett was a very good teacher and when the class worked hard, he would bring out his guitar and sing one of the modern top twenty hits that came to be called 'rock 'n' roll'. It wasn't unusual for anyone walking along the corridor to hear a class of twelve-year-olds belting out Bill Haley's *Rock Around the Clock,* but it never went down well with the 'real music teacher'. At the beginning I coped well enough with French and English but everything else went over my head. I had no idea what mathematics was about and science subjects totally confused me. So, by the time I reached the second year I was about to be demoted to a class known as 3FG, where basically all of those pupils who really should have stayed at Finnieston Primary were housed and some academic subjects were replaced by woodwork and metal bashing.

However, providence again intervened, in the shape of the French teacher, who argued that I was doing so well with French that I should be allowed to keep it on as a subject. Languages were not taught to 3FG pupils, who presumably were thought too thick to cope with them. His argument was accepted and I was moved to a higher class and ended up in a mixed class of boys and girls. Meanwhile he continued to play his guitar and he regularly sang a couple of Tommy Steele songs, 'Singing the Blues' and 'A Handful of Songs.' But even the presence of girls and pop music was not enough to motivate me to turn up every day and halfway into my second year I began to stay off as often as I could. When I did turn up, I received the belt on an almost daily basis either for talking back - defending myself as I saw it - or for failing to do homework. At one point I was given a homework book that had to be signed by teachers and others to 'prove' I had completed the tasks, but they eventually gave up on that as well. To a certain extent I was left to my own devices and these involved music, reading, cycling, playing football, swimming and by the age of fourteen dancing and playing snooker.

My interest in dancing arose firstly because it involved my first love, music and, secondly, girls. On the lead up to Christmas, physical training, or PT as it was known, was replaced by dancing lessons and we were taught the quickstep, foxtrot, waltz and other dances in preparation for the Christmas party in the school gym hall at the end of the year. I found out that the Locarno Ballroom in Sauchiehall Street had dancing sessions for young people on Saturday mornings, where they chiefly played modern records. I clearly remember my first visit on a Saturday evening when they had a live dance band. The noise from the live orchestra was deafening but an incredible sound. In the years that followed I became a regular visitor at most of the Glasgow Ballrooms: the Barrowland, Dennistoun Palais, the Plaza at Shawlands with its fountain in the middle of the dance floor. Within spitting distance of each other at around Charing Cross we had the Albert, the Berkley, the Westend Ballroom, the Astoria and the Locarno. In town there was Green's Playhouse, and a ballroom in Hope Street called the Majestic, but known to Glaswegians as the Magic Stick.

Many years later a university friend invited me to a pub in Ingram Street that had a live orchestra on Saturday afternoons. It did not have the same number of musicians as a dance hall band but they could certainly play. I asked my companion if she knew the singer and she said she did and during a break she shouted him over. I asked him what he had been doing in the early sixties and he told me he would think about it and came over during another break.

'I was singing with Ray McVey's orchestra in the Locarno.'

'I know.' I said, 'I was there listening to you. Tell you what I'll do,' I continued. 'I'll buy a drink if you sing a song today that you never sang in the Locarno over twenty years ago.' He just laughed and said it looked like he'd have to buy his own.

Margaret, my companion on that day, was a former classmate at Kilmarnock College who took up an offer from Stirling University to study for a degree in English. She graduated and became a teacher but before that she invited me up to Stirling for a look around the university. We were sitting in the refectory having some tea when she told me Dr Enid Marshall would be joining us. Enid Marshall was a very famous person in legal circles and taught law at the university. During my studies I had used many of her legal text books and happened to tell Margaret I found them pretty much jargon-free and easy to understand. Margaret, being

Margaret, mentioned it to Doctor Marshall when she met her at a reception in the university. She told her that I was a former truck driver who loved her books and had recently graduated. The doctor expressed an interest in meeting this particular fan, so Margaret arranged a meeting which was really why I was in Stirling. I presume she thought if she told me I was meeting with a famous writer on the subject of Scots Law I would not have turned up. She would have been absolutely right.

I looked up from our table and saw a rather thin, frail looking woman, with brown grey-streaked hair, and dressed in an all-black outfit approach our table.

'This is Doctor Marshall,' Margaret said, but I had worked that out already.

The good doctor suggested we go outside as it was a warm day and we sat on a bench near the river. We spoke about some of her books, which she thought were not well-accepted by some in the legal establishment but she was more interested in my lorry driving escapades. However, the conversation eventually turned back to the law. I mentioned that I had read in the *Daily Record* that the University had sought an interdict from the court, to prevent her bringing her dogs into the University. According to her view the University had sought the order through a court in Edinburgh rather that Stirling to try to avoid publicity. It was more likely that a local newspaper would have picked up on the story in Stirling but it would be missed in the busy civil and criminal courts of Edinburgh.

When we finished our talk, it was late in the afternoon and as she did not have a car, I offered her a lift home which she accepted. She directed me to an exit from one of the buildings and asked if I would pick her up outside in about ten minutes. As I waited in the car along with Margaret, I was browsing through some written material, when Margaret spoke.

24

'Here comes the doctor,' she said. 'She's got a dog with her.'

She got into the rear seat and sat there along with the dog. I looked in the rear-view mirror and caught her attention.

'I am really surprised that you are ignoring the interdict,' I said, 'but that looks awfully like a dog to me.'

She smiled and said, 'I would never ignore an order from the court but the terms of the interdict were quite specific. I was not permitted to bring two dogs into the University and sadly the other one died. My considered legal opinion is that the interdict died with her. If the University want to stop me bringing this dog in, they'll have to trot back to the court.'

She may have had 'the body of a weak and feeble woman,' but she had the heart of a lion.

Whilst Glasgow's dance halls became a regular haunt when I was in my early teens, I also became interested in the snooker halls. I first played snooker in a billiard room in St George's Road called 'The Nile.' It was a shabby, dingy place and the tables were old with stitches in the cloth, where some amateur had ripped the table with a cue. The roof leaked over some of them and the felt got soaked through when it rained. Nevertheless, I became quite proficient at the game and began playing for money around some of the Glasgow snooker halls, including the Imperial in Mitchell Street, the Royal in Maryhill Road, the Premier and Burroughes and Watts, both in Sauchiehall Street, and many others around the city. It was a gambling game and when I wasn't playing, I could also earn some money marking the board in games where the players were playing for money.

My interest in snooker came about as the family had moved from Oak Street to a two-bedroomed house in St Peter's Street near St George's Cross. The move meant I could return to live with my parents. So, despite my protests I left my grandmother's home for good and settled in the new house. It was quite a lonely time there because I didn't know anyone. One day I decided not to attend school and was looking for something to do when I noticed the stairs leading up to the Nile billiard room in St George's Road. I went inside and watched men playing snooker, an activity I had never seen before. After watching for a while, a man offered me a game and when he saw I couldn't hold the queue correctly, or do much else, he started giving me lessons on how the game was played and what the rules were. He turned out to be Barney Flanagan, who at one time was a Scottish amateur champion billiards player. He later invited me to the Premier snooker hall where he played billiards with his pal Mick McMorrin, a former Irish billiard champion. Billiards is only played with three balls whereas with snooker there are twenty-two balls on the table at the start of a match. However, the former enables a beginner to understand angles and ways of making the cue ball respond according to how you strike it. After a few weeks being coached and playing with Barney and Mick, my snooker game improved rapidly. In fact, I was a fair player when I was fourteen and won money gambling in the Glasgow halls. One night, a few years later when I had left school, I won twenty pounds in one match, which was the equivalent of eight weeks' wages. By then I had made new mates and I took them through to Edinburgh for the day. We went for something to eat in Woolworths on Princes Street, a few drinks in a pub on Leith Walk and finished up at an Edinburgh dance hall grandly entitled 'Les Edinburgh Palais de Dance,' and I still had money left for the café and juke-box on Sunday.

By the beginning of 1958 I had made friends with a number of boys from around the St. Peter Street area. Some of them had already left school and had jobs. Billy McKay was an apprentice typesetter with the *Evening Times*. Billy was famous for setting the advert for a film showing at the Odeon as 'Porky and Bess' when it should have been *Porgy and Bess*. Brian Baxter was an apprentice electrician and Ronnie McKechnie an apprentice motor mechanic. Ronnie worked with Wylie and Lochead's garage on Berkeley Street, where the owner of the white Rolls Royce, that was used for Grace Kelly's wedding, parked it overnight. Ronnie had keys to the garage and one night he 'borrowed' the Rolls and a group of us went for a run out to Milngavie and returned the car with no one being any the wiser.

Some older guys in St. Peter Street were bikers and most nights we would ride pillion with them over the Anniesland Switchback Road and out along the Great Western Road, but I never caught the bug. On my first attempt at riding a BSA Bantam, in a lane off Great Western Road, I throttled so hard and let the clutch out too fast causing the bike to spin straight up into the air and fall on top of me. To this day I've never liked motorcycles. On other evenings we would hang around the Royal Billiard Hall in Maryhill Road, where we would try and shark some unsuspecting punter into a game for money, so we could win enough to buy tickets for the Pavilion Theatre in Renfield Street.

Glasgow hosted a number of theatres in those days, the most famous being the Glasgow Empire, where allegedly ship's rivets were thrown at poor performers on Friday nights, when shipyard workers were in the audience. I find this rivet story a bit questionable and if you ever hold a ship rivet in your hand you'll know why.

My favourite story of the Empire is when Mike and Bernie Winters appeared there in the fifties, Mike came on alone and played the clarinet. He was dying a death so he waved his brother to come on to the stage to pull him out of a hole. When he did so a Glasgow voice was heard to shout above the silent crowd: 'Aw fuck! There's two of them!'.

In 1959 Cliff Richard also appeared at the Empire. None of the guys I hung around with liked him, preferring the four horsemen of the musical apocalypse: Elvis, Little Richard, Chuck Berry and Jerry Lee Lewis. Mickey, one of the older bikers, had bought a second-hand white American

Oldsmobile convertible with pink leather upholstery from a guy in Govan. It was a left-hand drive and could not pass a garage. One night during Cliff's appearance, about six of us bailed into this American gas guzzler and drove along Sauchiehall Street toward the Empire. As we approached the theatre a bunch of fans in the queue spotted the convertible with the roof down and assumed it was the man himself. They were sorely disappointed when they mobbed the car only to find six Glasgow blokes with hardly enough money for a gallon of petrol between them.

In the same year the American Academy Awards were shown on British television for the first time. It was different to see our on-screen heroes dressed in normal clothes and without their military uniforms or cowboy outfits. Two major cowboy actors featured prominently in the celebrations. Gary Cooper won the best actor award for his role in *High Noon* and was presented with his Oscar by John Wayne. This was quite ironic as John Wayne hated the movie and spoke out against the storyline that portrayed the men of the frontier town as cowards. In Wayne's view the settlers who travelled across the country would not have been fearful of a few outlaws.

Wayne later said: 'It's the most un-American thing I've seen in my whole life, for the rugged men of the frontier, who had battled the Indians as well as nature, would not be afraid of four villains. Instead, they would have united, as they had united to make the land habitable.' Maybe it was just sour grapes that he didn't get the part. Who knows!

Visits to the theatre were a regular part of Glasgow life and in the late fifties and early sixties I became a regular at the Pavilion, where Lex McLean appeared twice nightly. A crowd of us would heckle from our seats in the Gods but he always had the last word. He was an ardent Rangers' supporter and almost every night one or two of their players were in the audience and he didn't miss them if they'd had a bad game the previous Saturday. In later life he had a television series but his humour didn't really transfer from the stage to television.

I was twelve years old before I saw a television, apart from those on display in shop windows. My Aunt Margaret allegedly had one in her home in Apsley Street, but I never saw it during the time I visited, and as none of the family ever visited her, because she was married to a policeman, they never got to see it either. However, another Margaret, Margaret Callaghan, who stayed next door to my grandmother, bought a TV and immediately became very popular with the neighbours. It was in her house that I saw my first television programme. To be honest, I wasn't that impressed, preferring the radio, or the gramophone, but I do remember it was customary for people to watch the television with all the lights turned off. I can't remember when this practice stopped but I suppose it happened when colour television came along and the definition was improved.

By the end of 1958, we had a television in our house at St. Peter Street but I spent most of my time playing snooker, dancing or going to the football. I was a Rangers' supporter in those days and I would get the ferry from Finnieston Street to Govan with my pals and walk the rest of the way along Copeland Road to Ibrox. It must be admitted that we were mainly home supporters and when Rangers were playing away we would go to watch Partick Thistle, if they were playing at home.

My favourite joke that features Glasgow football bigotry tells the story of a Celtic supporter who finds himself in the Rangers' end at Ibrox. With his scarf hidden in his pocket he decides to keep his mouth shut and watch the game. It is 0-0, but just before the whistle goes, a Celtic breakaway leads to a goal. He gives the game away by cheering and when he realises what he's done makes a beeline for the exit. He is chased all the way along Copeland road until he crosses the

Govan Road and reaches the ferry steps. The ferry is about five yards away and he leaps from the stairs and lands on board. He looks up at the Rangers' supporters standing on the top steps and shouts: 'Away ya bunch of orange bastards.'

'You're taking a chance there, pal,' said the ferryman, 'this ferry's coming in.'

During the summer holidays the newspapers were full of stories about Peter Manuel, the serial killer, who was convicted of seven murders and sentenced to death. His execution was set for the 11th of July. I was compelled to go to Barlinnie Prison on the morning of the execution. I was fourteen years old and cannot explain why I went. Fundamentally I believe I thought capital punishment was wrong and I went in protest with many other citizens. However, the police at the gate were not interested in my views and promptly sent me packing, saying this was no place for a young boy. Perhaps they were right but it seemed to me, through reading newspaper reports, that there were doubts about the guilt of many people who had been executed. I had read about Derek Bentley, who was actually in police custody when his partner in the crime of burglary, Christopher Craig, shot police constable Sydney Miles on the roof of a warehouse in Croydon. The case hinged on whether the words: 'Let him have it, Chris,' claimed to have been uttered by Bentley, were meant to incite Craig into shooting the police officer. In later years it was claimed, by an officer at the scene of the crime, that these words were never said at all. Even if they were, I could never understand why Bentley was hanged when he was clearly not the shooter. Why our system put a politician in control of a person's life or death has always been anathema to me since those long-ago days. Manuel was clearly guilty but whether his death ever deterred a murder is extremely doubtful. I'd also read about the execution of Timothy Evans, a simple-minded boy who was in the wrong place at the wrong time, and never killed anyone. In fact, the killing of innocent people was quite a normal process in the days of capital punishment. Ruth Ellis should never have been executed. Her case was a crime of passion committed under severe provocation. These cases and others eventually led to the abolishment of the death penalty, but it was too late for those unlawfully killed by the State.

When I was growing up, hangings were rarely out of the newspapers. The records show that in the 1950s, over a hundred people were executed for murder in England and Scotland. Four of the executions in England were later held to have been miscarriages of justice: Derek Bentley, Timothy John Evans, George Kelly and Mahmood Hussein Mattan. The Mattan family became the first family to be awarded compensation for a person wrongfully hanged by the State.

Before the end of 1959 the school authorities had made it clear that I wasn't to be allowed to continue at school until I was sixteen. My attendance was bad and I wasn't doing well with most of the subjects. As we approached Christmas, I couldn't wait for the New Year to come. I knew I would be leaving school around Easter and no one would bother if I never appeared for classes, so I vowed to leave after the Christmas holidays and try and get a job.

As the last few days of 1958 drew to a close, the wooden floor of the school assembly hall creaked beneath the feet of the dancers whose attempts to waltz to Connie Francis's rendition of *Among My Souvenirs* were at best amateur, and at worst laughable. The only saving grace was that the efforts of the masters and mistresses to quickstep to Jerry Lee Lewis singing *Breathless* were patently worse. Nothing was in tune except the music. Fourteen and fifteen-year-olds tried to look and act twice their age. Heavily made-up girls tried to flirt with the male teachers whilst the boys, most of whom smelled as if they were sponsored by *Brylcreem*, were patronised by female teachers who were not averse to whacking them with a leather belt on other occasions. From

31

the first-floor landing I watched the scene below with more than a little embarrassment. At least I would not be returning after the holidays. I'd made my mind up.

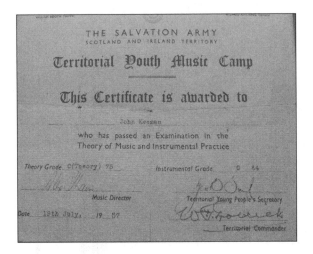

THE SALVATION ARMY
SCOTLAND AND IRELAND TERRITORY

Territorial Youth Music Camp

This Certificate is awarded to

John Keenan

who has passed an Examination in the
Theory of Music and Instrumental Practice

Theory Grade C(Theory) 75   Instrumental Grade   D   84

Music Director   Territorial Young People's Secretary

Date   18th July,   19 82

Territorial Commander

Chapter Three

Spies and the 1950s and 60s

Over the next few years, a couple of my mates got married, two joined the army and the rest of us carried on as usual. I had a number of girlfriends during that time but nothing was ever serious. In 1962 I went to see the great American rock star Jerry Lee Lewis at St Andrew's Halls in Glasgow.

Over forty years later I received an email from a lady in America who had emigrated to the United States in the 1970s. She said I had taken her to the concert and sent a photograph of her from around the time. Despite the image, I have no memory of her as a young girl or indeed having taken any girl at all to that concert. However, I do remember that when Jerry Lee walked on to the stage, he kicked the piano stool away and began to sing *Great Balls of Fire*. This caused everyone to leave their seats and dance in the aisles. Suddenly the music stopped and the house lights came on. An official from Glasgow Corporation took the microphone and made an announcement. The gist of this was that the concert would be cancelled if we did not remain in our seats. During his speech the piano stool had been replaced and after he left the stage the lights went down, and Jerry Lee walked back on, kicked the stool away and broke into song. Once again, the audience rose and began to dance and once again the lights came on and the wee man reappeared. This time he was followed by an entourage, who were clearly Jerry Lee's people. He made the same threat to cancel the show as before and walked off. I don't know what was said by Jerry Lee's people but he appeared for the third time, we all got

33

up to dance and the show ran its course. The following day's *Daily Record* referred to a riot at the concert.

Around that time one of my mates fell for a prostitute, who plied her trade at the coffee stall at Charing Cross. His much older, married brother went berserk and eventually broke them up. We knew the girls who worked the coffee stall and they would often lend us money until payday, so we could go dancing during the week. Despite what they did for a living they were good pals with our group and treated us as mates with nothing untoward going on.

Prostitutes featured heavily in the news in the early 1960s with the major scandal known as 'The Profumo Affair.' This saw the Tory Secretary of State for War, forty-eight-years old John Profumo, sleeping with a nineteen-year-old model, Christine Keeler, who was also kipping with a Russian 'Naval Attaché,' at the Soviet Embassy. Naval Attaché is a euphemism for Russian spy. Keeler and her friend, Mandy Rice-Davis, became two of the most famous models in the world. They were just a bit younger than me and I never understood at the time why such beautiful young women would tag along with these old men. I suppose it was the money and power thing. If Ian Fleming had written a story about a government minister sleeping with a model who was also sleeping with a Russian spy and an osteopath who was living off immoral earnings, his publisher would probably have told him it was too far-fetched. Profumo resigned from Parliament in June 1963, not because he played around with a nineteen-year-old but because he lied to Parliament about doing so.

Spies and spy rings were a regular topic for 1950s newspapers with stories about Klaus Fuchs, who gave the secrets of the Atomic Bomb to the Russians, and the Portland Spy Ring featuring Harry Houghton, Ethel Gee, Gordon Lonsdale and Peter and Helen Kroger.

Spies were everywhere including inside MI5 and the BBC. The United States had their spies too also but seemed to deal with them more cruelly than Britain. Whereas Britain sentenced Fuchs to fourteen years, of which he served nine, the United States executed Ethel and Julius Rosenberg for the same crime - passing secrets to the Russians. At home, Guy Burgess, who worked with the BBC for a time, and Donald Maclean, a British Diplomat, defected to the Soviet Union in 1987. It later transpired they were part of a network of spies, recruited at Cambridge University in the 1930s. The others that made up the Cambridge Five were Kim Philby, a high-ranking officer in British Intelligence; Anthony Blunt, Surveyor of the Queen's Pictures; and a Scot, John Cairncross, a civil servant who between 1941 and 1945, is alleged to have supplied the Soviet Union with over five-thousand secret documents. If ever there was a Thatcher's 'enemy within,' it was these guys and not some Yorkshire miners.

Spies, the atomic bombs and capital executions were regular news features during the fifties and sixties but near the end of 1963, Glasgow featured heavily in the news when the mail train from Glasgow to London was robbed in Buckinghamshire. The media dubbed it the crime of the century and the term 'master criminal' was thrown around haphazardly. In fact, it was an unmitigated disaster, with the gang leaving fingerprints and dozens of other clues at a farmhouse where they holed up for days. Most of the robbers were arrested quite quickly but one minor participant became a world personality when he escaped from prison and lived as a fugitive for over thirty years.

With train robbers and prostitutes, spies and a new Labour Government to gossip about around the coffee stall at Charing Cross, we were well served by the *Daily Record* and *Evening Times*, but more was to come before the year ended.

On Friday the 23rd of November the President of the United States of America, John Fitzgerald Kennedy, was assassinated. It is said that most people who were old enough to be around at that time, remember where they were on the day and I certainly do. I was in bed with the flu that Friday evening. I saw the news on television and was compelled to get up and go out to meet some friends, despite feeling like death. We met in the 'Owen Jones' pub at the bottom of Byres Road and our conversations turned to whether the Russians were involved and whether it would lead to a nuclear war.

We had come very close to a nuclear conflict in 1962 when the Russian President, Nikita Khrushchev, tested Kennedy's resolve by setting up missile bases in Castro's Cuba. But the young American held his nerve and his older adversary backed down. That same year Kennedy made a speech in which he said: 'We choose to go to the moon,' but he never lived to see it. I did, but I was never really that interested. It was a wonderful achievement, but a hell of a lot of money to spend on developing a non-stick frying pan.

Now, at the end of 1963, Kennedy was dead and many of us felt Lyndon B. Johnson could screw things up. A young American called Lee Harvey Oswald was killed whilst in police custody as the main suspect of the assassination. We'll never know whether he was indeed the assassin. For over fifty years, trillions of words have been written asking the same question: 'Who shot President Kennedy?' About the only group not blamed for the assassination so far is the Women's Institute. I read a book called *Rush to Judgment*, written by American lawyer, Mark Lane, after which I never believed Oswald was a lone shooter. Oliver Stone's movie *JFK* suggests there are more red herrings in the Kennedy assassination than there are in the North Sea.

In 1964, LBJ signed the Civil Rights Act into law but came under severe criticism for his handling of the Vietnam War. Students and other protesters surrounded the White House on a daily basis with shouts of: 'Hey! Hey! LBJ. How many kids did you kill today?' Within a few years the civil rights leader, Martin Luther King, would also die from an assassin's bullet, followed by JFK's brother Robert Kennedy.

My sister got married in 1964. It was quite a big affair with the wedding taking place in the Kent Road Church and the reception at the Grand Hotel, Charing Cross. After the meal we assembled in the large dance hall for the obligatory speeches. Afterwards, the two families sat facing each other in the large dance hall, while a three-piece band played away in the background. Nobody was getting up to dance so I went over to the band and asked them to play a few Sinatra numbers.

'We'll play them if you'll sing them,' said the guy on the piano so I took him at his word and after doing a few songs, I was dragged away, but at least it got them up to dance. Of course, as I explained to everyone, I had sung with a band before; although I conceded that the Salvation Army band did not swing as well as Sinatra. Singing was a normal activity for most people in those days. I could walk home from the Locarno and hear songs coming from the windows of the tenements in the early hours of the morning. *The Old Rugged Cross* and *The Wild Side of Life*, were very popular as was Tony Bennet's *I Left My Heart in San Francisco*.

The coffee stall next to the fountain at Charing Cross was opened throughout the night and many of the dancers would gather there after the five nearby dance halls closed: The West End Ballroom, the Berkeley, the Albert the Astoria and Locarno. One Saturday night my friend Wilma and her mates decided that business was quiet and they were going home. I offered to walk Wilma part of the way and when we reached St George's Cross, we stopped to talk with some people on their way home from the town. It was after midnight and they said they'd heard a noise coming from Divers pub on New City Road as they passed. My curiosity got the better of me as my mate Billy McKay had got a part-time job in the very same pub a few weeks before and was normally left in charge on Saturday nights.

I persuaded Wilma to come with me and when we arrived at the pub, just after midnight, the doors were closed but the padlock wasn't on. I pushed the door open and we went inside to find Billy and a load of other people having a party. We joined in and must have been there for a couple of hours before the police arrived and cleared the place. Pubs closed at half-past nine in those days so it took the police a while to catch on. Needless to say, Billy lost his part-time job, but it was a great night while it lasted and the beer was really cheap.

I travelled to my job as a message boy, at Farquharson Brothers, every morning on the number nine tram from Argyle Street into the town centre. One morning I noticed an attractive blonde girl at the stop. I was sure I had seen her at the Locarno the previous weekend. She was there every morning over the next few days and we got chatting and I asked her if she wanted to go to the pictures. A few nights later we went to a picture hall in Whiteinch to see Frank Sinatra in *Young at Heart*.

The following weekend I was in the Locarno with one of my mates when I saw her and her auburn-haired friend standing near the bandstand. I suggested to my mate that we ask them up to dance but he said he didn't like the look of the auburn-haired girl and would only agree if he could dance with the blonde. So, I asked her mate, and over sixty years later we are still together. Her hair isn't as auburn as it was but mine isn't exactly fair either.

Her name was Janet and we did all the usual things that young people did in those days: parties, dancing, cinema, clubs and restaurants. I remember shortly after we met, I asked her if she wanted to go to a jazz club after we came out of the Locarno one Saturday night. She said her parents expected her home by midnight so I offered to go with her to her house and ask them if it was okay for her to stay out a bit later, as the club didn't open until midnight. When we went into the house in Pembroke Street her father and mother were having a quiet drink and there was a bottle of whisky, sherry and some beer on their table.

After I'd explained that the club was only at the top of the road and I would make sure Janet got home safely, they agreed she could go. Just before we were about to leave her mother asked me if I would like something. Thinking I was about to get a glass of whisky I agreed and she handed me two roast beef sandwiches.

Janet worked as a tailor's cutter in a factory in the Candleriggs, near the old Glasgow fruit market and earned around eighteen shillings a week making uniforms for policemen, fire brigade and the military. Her parents were nice people and I got on well with her dad. When we had a drink with them on Saturday nights, her dad and I would argue for hours about politics, unions, religion, horse-racing, the war and anything else that took our fancy. I think we drove Janet and her mother nuts at times.

Her dad was unable to work full-time as the result of a tramcar accident. I remember he used to suffer severe headaches and was sometimes unable to get out of bed. When he was fit, he did a bit of home decorating and was a bit of a DIY expert. He did a lot of work on the first house Janet and I later moved into at 123 Kent Road, just round the corner from her parent's home. One of the bedrooms was directly above Jimmy Orr's betting shop and I could lean out the window and listen to the racing commentaries.

Her dad used to talk a lot about the times he worked in the spirit trade and eventually I began to think about leaving my job and getting a job in a pub. One Friday evening I saw an advert in the *Evening Times* for a barman at the Gazelle Bar in Linthouse near Govan. I applied, was successful and I arrived on a Monday morning to begin my training with the bar manager, Mick Cameron. He took me through the job, showed me how to pour a pint and use the spirit optics. By the time the bar opened at eleven I thought I had a good idea of what was required and served people as they came in without too much difficulty. It was very quiet with only about two or three customers at the bar and a couple of old guys playing dominoes in the corner so I kept myself busy cleaning glasses. At the stroke of twelve I heard the sound of a horn and suddenly all hell broke loose. What seemed to be the whole workforce from Stevens' shipyard across the road invaded the pub. The men were shouting for beers, whisky, pies with peas, pies without peas, nuts and cigarettes. I spent the next thirty minutes in total confusion. By the time they had left, the place looked like a bomb had hit it and I spent the rest of the morning cleaning up and washing a mountain of glasses. The pubs closed from half-past two until re-opening at five in those days and when it came time to close for the afternoon, I told the boss I didn't think I could handle the job.

He simply looked at me, laughed, and told me I'd done alright. He told me to go home and get something to eat:

'You only have to go through it all again at five o'clock,' he said. 'What are you worrying about?'

I don't know why I came back, but and as I turned the corner into Govan Road just before five there was a queue of men waiting to get in, so I went through it all again. But, as things go, within a few days I was fully broken in as a barman and it was probably the best way to learn. The customers were a mixed bunch. By and large they were hard-working guys, but there were a few wide men you had to keep your eye on.

One day we got a new toilet seat fitted and about five minutes after the plumber left some guy screwed it off and took it home. I couldn't believe anyone would steal a toilet seat but I learned fast that they would steal anything that wasn't screwed down and even some things that were.

The Gazelle Bar in Linthouse was the first pub to be granted a licence in what was until that time a 'dry area'. The shipyard owner always objected to having a pub in the area as he didn't want his workers drinking at lunchtime. After he died the new management didn't take the same strict approach and a licence was applied for and granted. It was rumoured that there was some crooked deal involved and a councillor went to jail for accepting a bribe, but I never established whether that was true or not until recently, when I found an *Evening Times* article showing a certain Baillie Inglis was jailed for eighteen months for it.

Matt McGinn wrote a song about it entitled *A' for a Pub Hoose Licence,* which includes the lines:

The licence is the thing we want, but don't have any fears,
A man I know will have a word in some o' the judges' ears.
As long as your pockets jingle you can come along with me,
We will speak tae Bailie Inglis, he's the very man tae see.

I was taken in hand by an old guy, Eddie, who had worked in pubs for years after he'd left the army at the end of the war. Eddie taught me cellar work and how to clean out the beer pipes and change barrels. This was relatively easy as the main beers, light and heavy, were pumped into four large tanks from a beer tanker. When one of the heavy or light was empty, I simply changed the pipes over and phoned the brewery for a refill. The tanker crew arrived, cleaned and sterilised the tanks, pumped in the beer from the street and it was ready to go. Denholm's, at the bottom of Hope Street, was the first pub in Glasgow to use Toby beer and the first to have a carpeted cellar. The other beers we sold, lager and Guinness, came in smaller barrels and I learned how to change them over when one or the other emptied. I was also charged to make sure the beer pipes were clean and given a small hand pump for this purpose.

After using this slow and not very effective system, I came up with the idea of using an empty lager barrel. I would clean it out then attach it to the pipes and blast a few gallons of water through the pipes using the gas. Firstly, I had to remove the siphon from the centre of the barrel which

41

was on a thread. I tried turning it with a large spanner but it wouldn't budge so I turned to using a hammer and chisel placed against the lugs. It eventually began to move and then the world went black! I was found lying unconscious on the cellar floor. I had not thought of pressing down the valve and letting the air out of the barrel and it was this that was making it difficult to screw out the siphon. Once it became loose the gas propelled it out like a rocket. It hit me square in the mouth, halved one of my front teeth, and knocked me out. However, the system worked and I never again forgot to release the gas before I washed the pipes and I reckon we had the cleanest beer pipes of any pub in Glasgow.

As Christmas approached that year, I was busy finding space in the cellar for all the extra stock when a whisky delivery arrived. The driver advised that he had fifty cases of a particular blend which I was convinced was a mistake. Normally we only ordered one or two cases of this whisky so I went to check with the owner.

'It's okay,' he told me. 'It's a special deal for Christmas and the New Year.'

When I asked how he expected to sell so much of this unpopular brand he opened a cupboard in his office and handed me a funnel. Over the weeks leading up to the holiday I spent most of my days decanting this blend into other bottles when they became empty. We had over thirty blends of proprietary whisky on optics and every one of them contained the same blend, regardless of what it said on the label. One Saturday morning two customers asked me for this blend and when I looked around the gantry it was clear I hadn't put one of the Christmas deal bottles on an optic. I had to tell the customers we didn't have any of that particular whisky when every bottle was full of it. Of course, they took something else and spent most of the time complaining it wasn't as good as their favourite tipple.

I worked at the Gazelle for about a year until I decided

I wanted more responsibility and a possible manager's job sometime in the future, so I began to look through the trade papers and other publications. I spotted an advert for a second hand in a bar in Clydebank and applied, and again I was successful. The bar wasn't far from a shipyard, which I believe was instrumental in my gaining the position, but it was never as busy as the Gazelle. There were plenty other pubs in the area but the charge-hand, who had worked in the Clydebank bar for about thirty years, didn't take any nonsense from anyone and I believe his attitude kept many customers away. However, the owner, a woman in her fifties, seemed to be happy with the profits she made, so nothing was done to change the situation.

I was in charge two nights a week when he was off so I began to get experience of running the place on my own, dealing with staff, banking the takings and so on. I also learned quite a bit about money lending in the shipyards and also in Singer's nearby sewing machine factory, particularly with regard to exorbitant interest rates. This pub was very quiet during the week and extremely violent at the weekends with the odd gun being produced. It was a real dead-end job and I was looking out for something more suitable and like other times in my life, providence took a hand.

At that time the pubs in Clydebank closed at two in the afternoon and nine in the evening, having different licensing laws than Glasgow where pubs closed at two-thirty and again at nine-thirty. The bar was quiet during the week and we could always get closed bang on nine o'clock. If I caught a tram right away, I could get to my local pub, the Two Ways Bar, or the Coffin End as it was affectionately known due to its shape, in time for a pint, before it closed at nine-thirty. As I regularly arrived in the bar just before closing time the owner, John Gordon, asked me one night why I always appeared during the last half-hour and I explained that I worked in a pub that closed at nine.

Over the next few months, we got chatting every night mostly about the pub business. During one of these chats he offered me a job as his bar manager. He explained that he was thinking of taking things a bit easier and was looking for someone to run the place so he could have most nights off. I had the gall to ask him if he intended being there any nights when I would be at work. When he said he would be, I asked him who would be in charge when both of us were working together. To my surprise he said that I would be responsible for making any decisions relating to staff, stock control, customer control and any other work-related matters.

I don't know whether it was my sister getting married that prompted Janet and me to consider doing the same. I can't remember who proposed and I think we just sort of grew into the idea but we were clear that it wasn't going to be a big affair. Neither of us were church goers at that time and we thought it hypocritical to get married in a church when we never attended one, so we agreed on a Registry Office marriage. On the 2nd of October 1965 we got married in Martha Street. I remember arriving wearing a dark blue mohair suit, a 5th Avenue Shirt, silk tie, winkle-picker shoes and sporting a black eye.

The black eye came about through confusion over a taxi in Byres Road the night before, with a couple of Irish builders. We were actually getting out of the taxi but the Irishmen thought we were trying to get in and a few punches were thrown. In the end the Irishmen joined us in 'Owen Jones' pub as the taxi drove off. The photographer's assistant at the Registry Office put some make-up around the offending eye and the photos don't look too bad over fifty years later. After the ceremony we had a meal at the Kenilworth Hotel in Queen Street, followed by a night at the nearby Pavilion Theatre, where Lex Maclean put the spotlight on our seats, but by that time we'd left and were sitting in Wilson's pub in Sauchiehall Street having a quiet drink on our own. We still have the bill from the Kenilworth which was around fifteen pounds. We hadn't made any plans for a honeymoon, but a woman in Janet's work had a holiday cottage at Rothesay which she gifted to us for two weeks as a wedding present and on the Sunday we travelled to Rothesay from Gourock as Mr and Mrs Keeman. I was twenty-one and Janet nineteen.

Janet and John's wedding 1965

Chapter Four

The Honeymoon is Over

After our two weeks in Rothesay we returned to our new home that Janet's dad had finished painting and decorating. It was a two-room and kitchen at 123 Kent Road with an inside toilet. We had the fireplaces bricked up and Gas Miser fires installed which meant there was no coal bunker, no making a fire first thing in the morning with wood and newspaper to get it started and no constant smell of smoke. We had some nice furniture, including a three-piece suite and a gramophone. The money for these purchases came from the Provident Cheque Company via furniture vouchers. A 'provy' cheque or vouchers were only accepted by certain shops and were an expensive way of buying goods on credit, but as long as we could continue working it looked like we were in a position to settle down to married life quite comfortably.

The motto of the Burgh of Govan is *nihil sine labore*, meaning you get nothing without working for it, and so it was for most people in Glasgow and elsewhere. I went back to my job at the Two Ways and Janet to hers at Moore, Taggart and Company in the Candleriggs.

I suffered a tirade of good-natured abuse from the customers on my first day back at work because I had outwitted them on the afternoon before the wedding. I was working on that day and I got an idea that some of the customers were planning a surprise such as tying me to a lamppost or some other embarrassing deed. I had arranged with Mr. Gordon to finish work at lunchtime, so just before then, I told him I was going to King's grocers, a few doors down, for a roll and gammon. I said this within hearing of the customers, some of whom asked me to get them a roll as well. I took their orders on a slip of till roll and left the pub in my shirt sleeves and wearing my apron. I never came back, but went straight home to get ready for my stag night later that day. When I returned to work, the customers insisted I buy them rolls that they'd paid for two weeks earlier so I was forced to oblige, but I'm sure one or two of them hadn't ordered or paid for a roll in the first instance.

There were some characters among the Two Ways' clientele: Joe Cadden owned a locksmith business and was often called on by the police to open locks. When he wasn't working, he could be found at the corner of the bar from opening to closing time. He had company in the shape of a local boarding-house owner, and a guy who seemed able to get you anything you needed very cheap: watches, suits, shoes, shirts, TVs, record players, women's clothes and jewellery. I later found out he was running a scam with catalogue companies, in addition to his own job as a joiner. He would rent a house for a month at a time and order as much stuff as he could from catalogues, newspaper ads, magazine ads and any other sources of buy now and pay by instalments. He would then move the goods to a lock-up and flog them cheap.

Joe lived with an Irish woman called Isa and they were constantly fighting and arguing. She was a big woman who could handle herself in a fight and I witnessed her flooring more than one guy who tried it on at the bar. She would come in some days at opening time and order a drink and cigarettes saying Joe was next door getting a paper and he would pay when he came in. She would swallow the whisky and beer and leave with the cigarettes and Joe would not turn up until hours later. When he did, he was asked to pay for what Isa had ordered earlier in the day and did so with the caution he would not pay the next time if she did the same thing.

There was no stunt Isa would not pull to get a free drink. When Joe's dog, a border collie, was having pups, he promised Janet the pick of the litter as a wedding present. I went round to the locksmith's shop with Janet and we picked one. A few weeks later Isa arrived at our house to deliver the pup and tried to get me to pay for it. I chased her. Another stunt she pulled happened when Joe sent her for a bottle of whisky when he ran out of drink during a session in the back shop of the locksmith. She bought a bottle from King's and on her way back to the shop she went into the Berkeley Bar for a quick drink. She sat down near some people who had come in for a drink during the Kelvin Bingo interval. One of them, a man, was speaking about having won a jackpot house and was overheard by Isa. Having sized up the situation she took a gamble and asked him if he wanted to buy a bottle of whisky cheap. He said he would and she handed over Joe's bottle and waited for the response she expected. 'Can you get any more?' he asked. Isa told him she could but he would have to give her the money and she'd go and get it. The man handed over the cash for three bottles. Isa hurried back to King's, bought a bottle for Joe and pocketed the rest of the man's winnings. We only found out what had happened when Isa was seen running away from the man a few days later when he spotted her from the bingo queue. His friends told everyone around what she'd done. Needless to say, he never caught her.

My favourite memory of Isa happened in the pub one night when I was behind the bar. Isa was a big woman and was standing at the bar wearing a black V-neck jersey which did little for her modesty. Two young guys, about ages with me at the time, were getting an eyeful and I heard one say to the other:

'Do you think they're real?'

Isa also heard the remark, put her hand inside her jersey

and pulled out her breasts:

'Do they fucking look real?' she asked, before putting them back.

I was quite shocked, but nowhere near as shocked as the two onlookers, whose faces lit up the whole pub. What a woman!

There was rarely a dull moment at the Two Ways. One night, the guy who ran the catalogue scam was drinking with Joe and some others. He stayed on the first floor of the tenement above the pub. When his tea was ready his wife would call out the window. This particular night she had called three times but he continued drinking at the bar. I heard a commotion at the door, that led out into Kent Road, and looked over to see his wife wrestling with a mattress. She finally got it through the door, left it in the middle of the floor and shouted:

'Why don't you just sleep in the fucking pub?'

I was about to come from behind the bar to reason with her but she walked out followed by roars of laughter. She was no sooner gone than she opened the door again and threw an alarm clock across the bar shouting at me:

'And you can get him up for his fucking work in the morning.'

I recall two shipyard plumbers both called Charlie, one Brown, the other McCabe. The latter splashed out on a new colour television for his eighty-year-old mother but she asked him to take it back to the shop as the programmes were not as good as those on her old black and white set. The two Charlies were rarely seen apart and arrived after work every weeknight and Saturday mornings to order 'two blacks and two blues.' This was two Black Label whiskies and two bottles of McEwan's Blue Label beer. One night, Charlie McCabe came in alone saying the other Charlie had to see some people in a pub in Clydebank. Just before closing time, Charlie Brown came in clearly the worse for drink. He was

49

so drunk that Betty, the waitress, refused to serve him, so he asked her to phone a taxi.

'Where are you going?' Betty asked.

He muttered he was going home. Betty then tried to explain to him that he only stayed above the pub but he didn't get it. I told Betty I would deal with him and phoned a taxi. When the taxi arrived, I told the driver just to drive him round the block and drop him off at his close and I would pay the standard fare. The driver obliged and when I tried to get the money from Charlie the next morning, he told me I must be stupid if I thought he ordered a taxi home from the Two Ways, when he only stayed up the stairs.

'Anyway, I wiznae in here last night,' he said. 'I wiz in a pub in Clydebank.' But it wasn't all fun.

Early one Saturday evening, my Uncle James came in after the football and was clearly drunk. I refused to serve him and he became quite abusive, particularly with some disparaging remarks about my boss, Mr. Gordon, who was at the other end of the bar talking with some customers. I knew my boss could hear what James was saying and again I told him to go home but he wouldn't budge from the bar. Out of the corner of my eye I saw the boss approaching. I stepped forward and told him this idiot was my uncle.

'You can pick your friends, son, but you can't pick your relatives,' he said.

With that he walked round the bar, picked James up by the scruff of his neck and threw him out the door. James was not by any criteria a small man, but John Gordon was built like the proverbial brick toilet and as strong as a horse. He was not a man to be messed with, which is why he ran such a successful pub.

Most of my time spent working in the Two Ways was enjoyable but being paid as a manager brought with it some unpleasant duties. One of the waitresses, known as Hielan Agnes, as she came from a mountainous area of Scotland

- which could be anywhere really - fell down the cellar steps one Saturday evening. She was not badly injured, but I determined it was the fact that she was drunk that saved her. On Saturday nights we were very busy and she spent most of the time serving in the lounge bar. There was a large contingent of highlanders who came in on Saturday nights and it transpired that the waitress was undercharging them for drinks. The custom was for bar staff to pool their tips and split the money between them at the end of the night. Hielan Agnes, who was in her fifties, rarely had anything to contribute. This, as I figured out, was because she took her tips in liquid form. In the end I discussed her behaviour with Mr. Gordon who asked me what I wanted to do.

'I have spoken with her about drinking when she's working but she won't listen,' I told him. 'Either we put up with it or fire her. I think we should fire her.'

His response sort of set me back a bit.

'Well, you're the manager so it's your decision.' he said.

After her shift on the next Saturday evening she was clearly drunk at the end of the night. I told her to come and see me on the Monday morning before we opened to discuss her work. When she arrived, she was not in a conciliatory mood and suggested she should be paid for the morning. I raised the issue of her drinking on duty, failing to share her tips with other staff and being quite drunk on occasions. I told her she was putting her job at risk but she just flew off the handle.

'You can't sack me!' she shouted.

But I'd had enough. I told her I could, and I was, and she could pick up the wages due her later that afternoon and a letter of dismissal would be sent to her home address. Then I asked her to leave the premises.

Shortly after she left, and just before I opened the pub for the day, I got a call from Mr. Gordon. He asked me how the meeting went and I told him I'd sacked her. I also told him she was coming to see him, as she didn't believe I could sack her. He assured me he would back me up and suggested I advertise for a replacement.

When I closed up for the afternoon, I was walking home when I met my mother. She started shouting at me in the street because I'd sacked Agnes, and she came out with one of her standard sayings:

'You're too smart for your own good!' She roared.

I'm not sure I ever understood that remark when I heard it. It seems to fit in with Billy Connolly's: 'You'll laugh on the other side of your face.'

I told her it was none of her business and walked on as if she was a strange woman who had accosted me in the street. But all good things must come to an end as the saying goes.

Some eighteen months after I started work in the Two Ways, Mr. Gordon took me aside and told me he had decided to retire and was selling the business. The new owners were to be Tennent's Brewery. He said he had negotiated with them to retain the present staff but they would not agree to the current wage structure. In particular they thought I was being paid a fair bit over the odds and also considered I was a bit too young to be a manager of one of their pubs. I was getting twenty-five pounds a week when Tennent's managers of pubs with a similar turnover were on eighteen pounds. He told me I would be interviewed and it was up to me how I dealt with the new bosses.

The day for my interview duly arrived and after listening to their management speak until I was fed up, I asked if I were permitted a question. They both nodded like a couple of wee dugs in the back window of a car.

'I expect you need a fair amount of intelligence to do your job. Would that be correct?' I posed.

They both nodded, again in unison.

'Then why are you so stupid as to offer me a demotion to second hand in a pub I've been managing for over two years and a cut in wages?'

I was quite wound up by the next suggestion when one of the Harvard Business School adherents piped up:

'Surely as an assistant manager you can always make your wages up …' he said.

'Are you suggesting I should steal my wages?' I asked, 'I wonder what your bosses would think about that idea if I asked them.'

He was turning a pale colour when I got up from the table in the lounge and joined my former boss in the public bar.

He had already set me up a large Bacardi and coke with a Carlsberg Light chaser.

'I knew you wouldn't take a job with them. You're not the type to work with a faceless gaffer and a rule book,' he said.

'The bastard suggested I could make up my wages. You know the sort of thing: water the Scotch, serve short measures, put the dregs of spirits into the black rum and the beer back into the drip tray.'

Everything I hated about the Gazelle and the Clydebank Bar. Ripping off your own kind.

'Pair of bastards! It won't work you know,' I said, 'over ninety percent of our customers drink McEwan's beer, heavy and light. They won't tolerate Tennent's heavy- it tastes like piss. They'll cross the road to the Sandyford Bar or go up the street to the Rex Bar.'

'Christ, I hope you didn't tell them that,' Mr. Gordon said, 'I tried to sell to McEwan's Brewery but Tennent's made the better offer.'

We both laughed and ordered up another drink. I saw Mr. Gordon some months later when he had bought a licensed grocer's shop on St. Vincent Street. Retirement wasn't for him.

A few days after leaving the job I was offered some work of a clerical nature with two customers of the Two Ways, Peter and Dougal, who worked as roller-shutter door installers for a company in Anniesland. When they installed a new door, they kept aside a few slats until they had enough to make a full door, which they would sell for some pocket money. On those occasions I was asked to print written quotations, simple contracts and receipts for which I was paid. This tided me over until I applied for a job as a manager of a licensed grocer in West Nile Street. I was successful in my application and during my time there I improved my communication skills as my customers included stars of stage, screen and television, priests, accountants and lawyers. A famous Glasgow gangster's lawyer was a customer, entertainers from the Pavilion, including Lex Maclean, who bought a bottle of brandy and a dozen Babychams every night. The famous duo of Francie and Josey, or Rikki Fulton and Jack Milroy, were also regular customers. Up the close next door was a theatrical agency run by a guy called Max who had Andy Stewart, among other Scottish acts, on his books. I got to know Lex MacLean quite well and would let him use the phone in my office when he needed it. He was a very pleasant man and dressed like a real gentleman with his soft hat and camel hair coat. I remember telling him I went to the show regularly and was there the night I got married.

'I hope you left early,' he said, laughing.

My favourite Lex McLean joke is one he told in the Rangers club one night. He read out a letter that he claimed came from a young man looking for advice:

'Dear Mr. McLean,

I am 32 years old and have two brothers. My older brother works for Willie Waddell and is an ardent Rangers' supporter and the other is in Barlinnie for arson and rape.

My father lives off my sister's earning as she has a good pitch in Bath Street. My mother is having a baby to the next-door neighbour and for this reason my father won't marry her. I have met a charming girl whom I want to marry. Do you think I should tell her about my brother, the Rangers' supporter?'

The company who owned the licensed grocers also ran the Market Inn hotel, just off the Gallowgate, and I kept close to my working-class roots by working there on Sundays behind the bar. I remember a customer who drank triple banana-rums washed down with pints of Guinness. I kept expecting him to throw up, from the smell of the banana rum alone, but he never did.

During my time in the grocers I enrolled for a Glasgow Corporation licensed trade course. It was designed for people who intended to go into management of pubs, clubs, hotels and other licensed establishments. It was a series of lectures and practical demonstrations but it was certainly not as boring as that sounds. In fact, almost every demonstration involved sampling the products and we usually staggered home at the end of the day. We visited breweries, distilleries, and other establishments in the spirit trade including Gaskell and Chambers, who sold bar fittings, optic measures, tumblers, beer fonts and everything else you needed to run a pub. At their warehouse on London Road they had a mock bar set up but the drink was real. At the end of the course we were given a certificate stating we had studied licensing laws and other appropriate legislation, cellar management, hygiene, weights and measures and a few other areas. In fact, we had drunk ourselves silly for a week.

I had a few Catholic churches on the books for orders of communion wine that I purchased from Bulloch and Lade, a whisky and wine merchant in Waterloo Street. When I tried to place an order for two cases of communion wine one week, they could not supply it due to a dock strike. When the priest arrived on Friday morning as usual, I explained there was no communion wine available due to the strike. He asked if I could recommend an alternative and I opened a bottle of Eldorado Tawny, which in those days was a cheap wine favoured by Glasgow jakeys and commonly known as LD. I offered him a glass which he accepted and described as not unlike the communion wine he bought each week. He asked for two cases which I helped him load into his car. When I told him the price, he commented that it was considerably cheaper than his usual order. In fact, it was less than half the price. The following week he called me and ordered another two cases. I told him the dock strike was over and I could get his normal wine but he said he'd give the Eldorado a try for a while.

On the Saturday of the World Cup Final in 1966, I took my rented television into work in a taxi to watch the game. I had a bet on West Germany but we all know the history. The English haven't stopped talking about it for over 50 years. I wrote a piece, that the *Daily Record* printed, saying that English sports journalists suffered from a rare form of Tourette's Syndrome that caused them to constantly talk about the 1966 final. The England result was disappointing enough, but even worse news came the following week when Janet phoned me at work to say our house had been broken into when we were both at work. I got a taxi home immediately, to discover the gas meter had been emptied, all our record albums were missing along with a silver tea service, which once belonged to Janet's grandmother, and some other small items. We were at least thankful that the crooks did not trash the place and the insurance took care of our losses.

However, there was one aspect of the break-in that really annoyed me at the time. The Gas Board sent me a bill for the money missing from the meter which I refused to pay. I advised them that as I did not have access to the meter and had taken reasonable steps to secure my house, it was their loss, not mine. I told them to go ahead and sue me. Sometime after I sent the letter, a man arrived from the Board to check the meter that had already been repaired. We thought little of it until later that night the gas fire went out.

'I thought you put money in the meter earlier?' I asked Janet.

'I did. When I came in from work,' she said.

She put another coin in but it was not long before it ran out again. Then the penny dropped. The guy from the gas board had altered the tariff so we got less gas for our money, in an effort to recover the missing money. The eejit had re-set the meter far too low and it was obvious we were not getting very much gas for our shilling. I presumed the idea was that once they recovered the stolen cash the gasman would re-appear to 'check' the meter, and reset it to the correct tariff.

I went to their head office in George Square and confronted them with the evidence which they neither admitted nor denied but said a man would come and check the meter again. In a few well-chosen words, I told them I had more respect for the bastards who'd broken into my house than for the Gas Board. When the guy arrived and re-set the meter, he also got an earful and I told him to tell his bosses to send some other guy when the next meter check was due.

Sometime in early 1967 I began to think about moving on to something more interesting than wrapping up bottles of wine to make them look like a loaf, as one female customer used to request. I turned again to the newspaper adverts and found that The Gramophone Shop, situated on Argyle Street across the road from the Two Ways, was looking for a clerk. My application was accepted and I started my new job a couple of weeks later.

I worked downstairs in the basement where the walls were lined with hundreds of second-hand 78rpm records, mostly classical music. I was shown how to use an offset printer, which was a messy machine that needed loading with ink regularly. I used the machine to print off a catalogue of records for sale which was sent to customers in the UK and overseas. When orders arrived back, I arranged for them to be shipped to the customer. At the end of the day I loaded the parcels into the shop's car and was driven to the Sandyford Post Office from where they were sent on their way.

The business was owned by George Melvin and I later found out that, as a young man, he was pretty much uncommunicative. Various therapies were tried to get him to communicate with little success until he was introduced to classical music, in which he developed an interest. Quite naturally, his relatives and friends bought him records until his bedroom at his home in an Argyle Street tenement was virtually filled up to the ceiling. His mother suggested he noted down what he wanted to keep, set aside the best copies of the many duplicates, and advertise the rest for sale. The response he got to his advertisement was phenomenal and soon he was running a business from his bedroom. With the success he was having he came up with the idea to advertise that he would buy collections. Again, he was overwhelmed by the response.

By the time I started working for him he owned three shops: The Gramophone Shop, the Christian Book Shop next door, managed by his older brother, and a third shop in Byres Road that sold second-hand modern records. George worked in The Gramophone Shop himself along with two salesmen, Selwyn, a very heavyset Jewish man in his thirties, and Gordon, a Wagner fanatic. When George went home for lunch *Tannhauser* trumpeted throughout the shop. In June 1967 Selwyn had been missing for a few days so I enquired if he was off sick. 'He's away to Israel to fight in the war,' I was told. That turned out to be the Six Day War and I never saw or heard of him again.

I learned quite a lot about classical music and began to enjoy some of it, but my preference still lay squarely with Elvis, Jerry Lee Lewis, Chuck Berry and Little Richard. With Selwyn gone I was asked to take on a bit more work upstairs in the shop when my catalogue duties were complete, until the next catalogue was due. This meant answering enquiries by letter and telephone which normally involved some research which I enjoyed. One day I was asking George some questions in order to answer a letter, when he came out with a remark that got me thinking. He said it was a pity I didn't have a driving licence as he could use me to drive him about when his brother was on one of his off days. He was talking about his brother who ran the Byres Road shop but had a severe problem with alcohol. This meant that on occasions he would go missing for days and could not drive George to his appointments around the country to buy collections of records that customers offered for sale. These had to be rearranged which did not suit George or, indeed, his customers.

On hearing this, I resolved to take driving lessons. I booked a number of lessons with Dickie's Driving School on St. Vincent Street and began to learn to drive in a pale-blue Ford Anglia and was hooked from day one. I passed my test first time at the Springburn Test Centre and could not wait to tell George.

The business car was a Humber Snipe estate car, fully automatic, which was a beast of a machine next to an Anglia. After some persuasion George, who did not drive himself, allowed me to drive myself to the post office every day. Of course, I found other reasons for using it, mostly business but some personal. However, on one trip to the post office, I crashed into a security van on Argyle Street. The crew of the van thought they were being robbed and would not come out of the van until the police arrived. When the police did come, they determined it was the security driver's fault for creeping up Argyle Street on the wrong side of the road.

After a few weeks George asked me if I would drive him to England on a business trip. He had organised a list of customers who had indicated they had collections to sell and the first was in Selby, Yorkshire, where we stayed overnight. We next stayed at the Sherwood Inn in Nottingham, the Lion and Lamb at Brentwood, London, and a hotel in Chester on the way home. We were gone for about nine days and by the time I arrived home with an enormous teddy bear I bought in Southport for my weeks-old son, John, I knew my new career as a long-distance driver was beckoning.

Pavilion Theatre, Renfield Street Glasgow

Chapter Five

Driving for a Living

Getting a job as a lorry driver was not as easy as I imagined because most haulage companies preferred something called experience and at this stage, I had only ever driven two cars, a Ford Anglia and a Humber Super Snipe, one a manual gear shift, and the other an automatic. I tried for a job as a van salesman with Bilslands Bakery in Hydepark Street to get some experience of larger vehicles. I was accepted and consequently left my job at The Gramophone Shop. Following some training as a salesman I managed to drive a number of large vehicles with only one or two hiccups.

Sometimes, even to this day, I can still smell the aroma of the new baked bread that met you when you walked down the ramp into the bakery around five-thirty in the morning. If I am really lucky, I can sometimes taste the hot rolls dripping with butter that I had for breakfast every morning. I wasn't much of a salesman and did not earn much by way of commission, but I learned to drive large trucks and got experience of an articulated vehicle when I worked the night trunk to Dundee when the regular driver took sick. On his return I was given the Anderston district as my regular run.

Glasgow Corporation was beginning to demolish much of the area, lots of people were moving out, and the corner shops were not as busy as they had been previously so I had few sales. On one cake promotion deal the bakery were giving a fifty percent commission on sales of quite expensive, large sponge cakes. I convinced one customer to take a couple of dozen on a sale or return basis. I piled them up on the counter

61

and every day I noticed the pile never got any smaller. After a week or so the shopkeeper asked me to take them back and refund his money, which I couldn't do. I had already paid it into the bakery and received my commission. I said I would change them for fresh ones and told my van boy to take them out to the van. When I followed him outside, he reminded me that we did not have any new sponges and I told him just to wait a minute and take the old ones back in which he duly did. I went back into the shop and whilst the boy was rearranging the cakes the shopkeeper was obviously taking a more than passing interest until finally he spoke:

'You think you are a smart bastard,' he said, and pointed to the fact that he had initialled all the boxes.

It took some persuading to get the bakery to refund his money and they were not slow in taking back the commission. But many months later I had the last laugh with the shopkeeper.

I was no longer working with Bilslands at the time but one Sunday afternoon I was giving a mate, Jackie Lamont, a hand at his work. He was a driver with Burgess the butcher in Elderslie Street, near the Dorset Bar. The owner, Ian Burgess, was installing some new machines in his cellar below the shop and we were assisting him. When we had finished, he gave us the price of a beer, some butcher meat and asked us to get rid of a breadboard filled with pies that were just about to go off. Jack suggested we throw them in the midden or feed them to the ducks in Kelvingrove Park, but I had a better idea; sell them to the local corner shop. The owner did not know I had left Bilslands so he thought he was getting a bargain at threepence each. Some weeks later we were going to a party up above his shop and I inadvertently went into the premises for cigarettes and when he spotted me, he went into his 'smart bastard' routine. This time he didn't get a refund.

My van boy at Bilslands was an Indian called Ahmed. When it came to hard work, he put most adults to shame.

By the time I arrived at the bakery in the morning he had the van stocked and the paperwork concluded, ready to move out, but one morning he wasn't there. I stocked the van myself and I had just finished when he arrived to tell me he had been awake most of the night with a painful stomach. I told him that if he did the three big stores in the town with me first, I'd drive him home and do the rest of the run myself. I was parked on the right-hand side of Union Street facing south outside Massey's grocery. We had just finished the delivery and I was about to drive off across the street. It was raining and I couldn't see much in the wing mirror on the passenger side where Ahmed was seated. I asked him if it was okay and he said yes, I pulled out and hit a car, caving in its wing and part of the driver's door.

'For fuck's sake,' I said, 'why did you say it was okay?'

'I thought you were asking about my stomach,' he said.

Over the coming weeks I was getting nowhere with sales and the possibility of getting a job doing straight deliveries from one bakery to another, like the overnight trunk to Dundee, really depended on someone dying. I couldn't balance the books as well as I'd done as a coalman's tick boy and I eventually left after a short, but heated, debate with the personal officer over money I'd 'borrowed' to buy a tape recorder.

I heard the Glasgow Hiring Company at Port Dundas were looking for drivers and I applied and was offered a job with the van section. Following an argument with the foreman at my interview, he agreed to assign me to the heavy haulage section that I'd asked to work with in the first place. During this period, I learned to rope and sheet flatbed lorries, secure loads of steel with chains and dwangs and drive a 'trombone' - a lorry with an extending chassis that could be pulled out to handle very long loads such as lengthy steel pipes. However, the wage structure was such that there were different rates of pay according to the type of vehicles a driver drove each week. I could be driving heavy haulage vehicles for three days, and as long as I was put into the van section for a couple of days, the lower rate of wages applied. I spent a long time arguing over this which resulted in my being allocated the worst paid local driving jobs on the firm's books.

Two jobs in particular come to mind. The first was running the leftover waste from tobacco plants from the Wills cigarette factory on Alexander Parade. These organic materials were put into enormously large bags and were driven to the coup at Easterhouse. During each trip I was accompanied by Customs and Excise officers who insisted that each load was tipped and covered over in their presence. Apparently, this was to ensure that tobacco, on which no tax had been paid, was not recovered. Of course, once the Customs Officers had left the scene the workers dug the stuff back up again and separated whatever tobacco they could from the waste and I'd get my share the following day.

Another job also involved working with officialdom this time in the shape of the CID. One week each month I was assigned to a contract with the British Oxygen Company at Polmadie. My job was to follow two Glasgow detectives to farmhouses, garages, lock-ups and other small business premises in and around the city. Their aim was the recovery of stolen oxygen bottles, which were expensive things to make. The CID always had a list of places to visit and never charged anyone unless they got stroppy. I would then load the bottles on to the truck and follow their car to the next stop. They were okay guys and would buy me lunch when they had theirs. They usually stopped early in the day but told me not to deliver the bottles to British Oxygen until later and signed my sheet to ensure I got a couple of hour's overtime.

Another short-term contract was with the Gas Board. They had renewed all the gas meters in the Blackhill housing scheme and our job was to pick up the old meters and return them to the depot. It was quite a rough area and when I drove through one street a crowd of kids started throwing bottles under the truck wheels. I stopped the truck and shouted at them to cut it out when a voice came from a window above:

'Leave the weans alane. They're only playing.'

Around the corner I went to a first floor flat to collect a meter. The door was open and a voice told me to come in. I walked through the lobby following the voice until I reached the living room door and was invited in. A guy was parked in an armchair drinking from a bottle of Eldorado and smoking a roll-up.

'The meter's in the toilet on the left as you get to the front door,' he said.

On my way in I'd noticed there was a hole in the wall next to the living room door. In passing I asked if he couldn't get the Corporation to fix it?

'I did that,' he said. 'I'm no getting up every five minutes to let a fucking dug oot.'

I met another driver at the Hiring Company, John MacGonagle, who stayed above the stables on Kent Road just across the road from my house. I discussed the anomaly of wage rates and the fact that I felt I was being ripped off every week by being on heavy haulage for three days and then back on the smaller vehicles for the other two.

'That's because you don't bung the foreman,' he said. 'If you slip him a couple of quid, he makes sure you get four days on the heavy haulage and whatever overtime is going.'

'He's getting fuck all from me,' I insisted.

'Please yourself,' John said, 'but all the older guys are at it. That's how they get the long-distance work.'

I never attempted to go down that road and continued working at whatever job I was allocated and continued to complain about the system. After numerous attempts to get the workers to rectify this anomaly and an altercation with the boss in a Springburn pub, I was fired and on the lookout for another job.

Whilst seeking full-time work I supplemented my unemployment pittance as a board marker in my local bookies on Saturdays. This usually meant that when I went to collect my wages, Pat the bookie would tell me I owed him money, as I had a few bets whilst marking the board. I also worked as a tile-fixer's mate, taxi driver, window cleaner, and coal carrier.

I was also getting some work as a driver/skivvy with Watsons, a catering company in Kent Road. I got a shift one Saturday night when the company did the catering at a community hall in Bearsden for a cycling club. The club were entertaining French cyclists but unfortunately the gaffer turned up and caught me dancing with one of the guests when I should have been supervising the delivery of the food, tables, chairs, furniture and flowers for the function. He wouldn't pay me for the night so I had to borrow money from one of the workers to pay my bus fare home as he told the other staff anyone who gave me a lift would be fired.

I heard through the grapevine that Forth Caledonian, a large haulage company in Duke Street, was looking for delivery drivers so I applied and was engaged. As this was a fair bit away from where I stayed, I bought a second-hand car - a black 1952 Standard Eight. It cost me a fiver from a guy who lived in Victoria Road but it ran okay.

It was stolen twice from outside the haulage depot. The first time I phoned the police and they told me to come to the station and fill in a form. A question on the form asked the value of the car and I wrote 'five-pounds'.

'Is it an insurance job?' the comedian copper at the desk asked.

When I returned to the depot at the end of my shift the next day the car was back where I'd left it. Everything was okay and it started first time, so I phoned the police and told them it was back, in case I was stopped when driving it home later that day. The next day the car was gone again. I called the police and again was asked to come to the station. It was the same copper but he wasn't feeling as humorous this time as he'd torn up the first form and had to write out another one. The car was again returned to the same place, but this time the car thieves had put water in the petrol tank and sprayed some parts of the bodywork with blue paint. When I got the car towed home, I discovered that one of the thieves had left a jacket in the back seat and when my mate and I went through the pockets we found his unemployment card with his address. The initial reaction was to go round to his house and have a quiet word but we turned it over to the police and they went round in the early hours of the morning instead. I replaced the Standard with a Hillman Minx that cost me thirty quid and which got me to work on time every morning.

Small deliveries with Forth Caledonia were a nightmare. You never got to the point when your lorry was empty and every now and again the loaders would empty what was there and arrange for it to be delivered in small vans. Some of the parcels had been up the front of the lorry for weeks and if there was anything perishable the stink was sickening and I was looking for a change. Driving trucks for a living brought certain hazards with the job. If you delivered high value goods, like whisky or cigarettes, you were a potential target for hi-jackers.

A fellow driver I knew was hi-jacked on a lay-by on the old Glasgow to Edinburgh Road. He was flagged down by a woman who had apparently broken down. When he jumped down from his cab, he was overcome by three men. They bundled him into the back of the lorry and tied him up. An hour or so later they unloaded the cigarettes into another vehicle in a disused railway station in Edinburgh, told him to wait at least thirty minutes before shouting for help and made their escape. Of course, when this happened the police usually started from the assumption that the driver was in on it and my mate was put through the wringer before they accepted that he had nothing to do with the theft.

I fell foul of the police more than once when goods went missing from my lorry. They interviewed me a few times but it was a waste of their time and mine. When they finally accepted that a large number of workers had access to the trucks after they were loaded by nightshift porters, I was free to go. However, I figured they were so fed up with the number of unresolved thefts from that particular depot they would not let up. Unfortunately, I was correct and early one Friday morning I opened my front door in response to knocking and was pushed aside by four men who turned out to be detectives from Eastern CID. They carted me off in Ford Cortina to their office. Once there they began questioning me about various goods that they had retrieved from a house in the east end of the city, saying they had a witness who claimed I had sold them to the occupant of this Aladdin's Cave. I kept pointing out that many of the stolen items they showed me were not goods that my company delivered, so how could I have sold them to anybody? It became clear, however, that I was wasting my time so I just refused to say anymore. I was kept in overnight and, along with other prisoners, shipped to the Sheriff Court in Ingram Street on the Saturday morning. I was kept in a cell below the courtroom and kept insisting that I wanted to call my home to tell my wife what was happening. At last they agreed and asked for a number. I did not have a telephone at home in those days but could have given them the number for Janet's sister who stayed upstairs. However, I figured if she wasn't at home the police would say that I'd had my call so I gave them the number of my local pub, the George Bar on Pembroke Street.

I spoke with a mate and asked him to get someone down to the court with bail money and to contact a lawyer for me. In court the lawyer did not turn up and neither did the guy with the bail money. I spoke with a Legal Aid lawyer appointed by the court. I did not like his manner at all but he made a 'not guilty' plea and requested bail. Bail was granted but with no one there to pay it, I was carted back down to the cells and eventually transported to Barlinnie Prison, or Bar-L, as it was known by Glaswegians. I went through the whole 'dug box' process and eventually was locked up in a cell. I was told that if someone arrived with the bail money I could go home, but by seven in the evening, I was still waiting. Around half past that hour I heard the sweetest words I'd heard in a long while: 'Bail for Keeman!' The officer was shouting it at the top of his voice as he approached my cell. I was told later, by an old lag, that they did that to upset the other prisoners who were not getting out. I was taken down to the main gate where my mate was doing the paperwork and handing over the cash.

'Where the hell have you been?' I asked him.

'I ran some guys to the Cup Final in the minibus and picked them up after the match,' he said, 'it was all arranged before you got lifted.'

I told him that I'd been in one cell or another for the past thirty hours and my lawyer had not appeared in court, as his son was playing rugby for Scotland.

'Take me to the Central Station,' I said.

'Why? Where are you going?'

'For a fucking shave and a bath. The station is the only place I know where you can get a bath at this time on a Saturday night, unless you're a toff with a bath in the house.' I swear that after the bath I drank the best pint I had ever tasted. Over the coming weeks I was re-united with my lawyer and the whole episode was eventually resolved.

Of course, when the police weren't suspecting you of organising a hi-jack or things to fall off the back of your lorry, they were busy checking log sheets or hiding behind bushes to catch you speeding. I did not much like the police in those days - I never met a driver who did, but my view changed as I got older and had a grown-up family of my own. I suppose they had their job to do and I had mine. I was charged with speeding and log-sheet offences quite regularly as a young driver but I accepted this went with the territory. Employers expected you to get the job done and if you couldn't handle it then out you went. I gave up the job with Forth Caledonian following my run-in with the law and went to work with a company in East Kilbride.

Scotbeef delivered meat to butcher's shops, in the form of animal carcasses, around Ayrshire and the Glasgow area but it wasn't long before I was on the move again. Handling meat carcasses every day did not endear you to your wife and friends and no matter how many baths you had there was a lingering smell of animal fat and the stink got into the back of your mouth and throat, so you could taste it every time you ate or took a drink.

My next job came about when a dump truck driver I knew told me that a company called Foulis Plant Hire, based in Partick, were looking for a driver to deliver to building sites. I found their address and called in at their premises the following day. The boss gave me a driving test around South Street and, happy I was able to handle a flatbed truck, gave me a start. Foulis hired out anything and everything used on a building site: dump trucks, compressors, bulldozers, jackhammers, lighting, drills and tools of all descriptions. The truck had two steel ramps that you manually handled to load whatever machinery you were delivering or taking off hire. I got a mouthful a couple of times when I was caught driving a dumper truck up the ramps instead of using the winch. The trucks were fitted with personal radios and you had no sooner finished a job when the fat radio-controller was on the blower with another. I came in one morning to find no one had turned up for work, but a note was on the steering wheel of my truck. It said the office staff were at a meeting, gave me details of a building site in Stirling and told me to deliver the compressor, burning gear and burner. A compressor, gas bottles and hoses had been loaded into the back of the truck so I set off. I was driving up Byres Road a few minutes later when the walkie-talkie crackled into life. I tried to answer the call but I really couldn't make out a word that was being said so I decided to hell with it, switched it off and headed for Stirling. About forty minutes later I was overtaken by a car I recognised as my bosses' and quickly turned on the radio to hear my gaffer's voice telling me to pull into the next lay-by. When I pulled to a stop, two men got out of the car and walked toward me. I rolled the window down and recognised the gaffer but not the other guy.

'This is the fucking Burner,' the gaffer said.

It wasn't long after this incident that I was on the lookout for another job.

Whatling's Construction was beginning to build the approach roads to the Kingston Bridge a few hundred yards from my house. I had a mate who was an auditor with the company and he put in a word for me and I was engaged as a tipper driver. The work was okay and the money was good but you were kept at it and there was no time for slackers. Trucks were loaded with muck on the north side of the river at Charing Cross and driven over the Kingston Bridge to the Kingston dock on the south side, where the load was tipped into the Clyde as part of filling in the old dock. The bridge was not open to the public at that stage so we could manage three or four loads an hour. On a twelve-hour shift that meant one lorry shifted about five-hundred tons of muck and clay every day.

One day my mate Andy and I decided to have our lunch in a hut that was situated at the east side of the dock which had already been filled in. As we were sitting outside, another driver, Jit Singh, appeared with a load and reversed to the edge of the tip. Instead of waiting for the bulldozer driver to come back from lunch and open his back door he decided to do it himself. We watched as he got out of the cab and opened the back door of the truck. He went back inside the cab, engaged the lever that operated the tipper, jumped out and started walking toward the hut. As the tipper's body rose into the air the edge of the tip started to collapse and we could only watch as the lorry slid down and disappeared into the Clyde. A decision was taken to leave it where it was as it was too expensive to move an RB22 Crane from Charing Cross and have about twenty-five trucks doing nothing for days. Recovery would have resulted in financial penalties being applied. As far as I know the lime green tipper is still there below the houses that were built on the old dock.

Andy and I witnessed another interesting sight from the hut late one Friday afternoon. We had decided we'd had enough for the day and parked our trucks at the side of the hut where they could not be seen. Fewer and fewer trucks appeared as the drivers finished for the day and we were just about to leave when we spotted the foreman's truck coming into the dock. The bulldozer driver was with him and we were intrigued as to what was going on. It soon became clear when the gaffer tipped up an enormous pile of copper cable and the 'dozer driver jumped into his 'dozer and started covering it up with earth. He parked the bulldozer on top and jumped into the lorry as it drove off.

'Can you drive a bulldozer, Andy?' I asked.

'Naw, but I'll have a good go at it.'

After a good few attempts, we managed to get it started using a nail in the ignition and proceeded to dig up the copper. We wrestled with it and finally got it secured on the end of the bulldozer's blade. Andy lifted it as high as the blade would go and I raised the tipper and reversed under it. We managed to pull it into the truck and drive to a scrap yard in Scotland Street where the guy unloaded it with a crane and paid us a fair amount of cash. We were not working that Saturday but on Sunday we watched the gaffer and the dozer driver almost dig up the whole dock trying to find it. It ended with them both blaming the other for stealing it on the Saturday. Janet and I had a great weekend with our pals and their wives that weekend. Scrap was a major source of making some extra money on the site with enormous cast iron pipes being unearthed almost every day along with copper and aluminium cable.

Chapter Six

One Job After Another - the 1970s

It was the early 1970s and we had another son, James. Janet was now a full-time housewife and with only one wage coming in things were a bit tight, but she was always good at making ends meet and we still had an exciting social life with lots of friends. I knew there was still a few weeks' work left in the job but you never know what's round the corner. We had filled in the dock and were running the muck to a site on Maryhill Road. On the way to the tip I went into a betting shop on Bilsland Drive to use the toilet and parked the truck outside. When I came out, I found the doors of the truck locked and one of Whatling's managers sitting in his Vauxhall Victor across the road with a smug look on his face. He refused to hand over the keys unless I listened to his rantings, so I jumped on a bus and picked up my wages and holiday pay from the site after an argument with the wages clerk. I went home, handed what I had in cash to Janet and told her not to worry, I would get another job pretty soon.

Soon came quicker than I expected as I had a visit from the site boss in charge of the work on the Kilmarnock bypass who'd heard of my predicament. He needed three experienced tipper- drivers urgently so the following morning myself, Andy and another driver, John MacKay, were picked up at Glasgow Cross with a mini-bus and bussed to the site. Our first day was spent ferrying new Bedford trucks from Watson's garage in Airdrie to Whatling's site in Kilmarnock. I delivered five different trucks to the site that day and I remember every one of them handled differently. The job was standard muck-shifting and everything went well enough for the next few months until I noticed my lorry seemed to be using a lot of fuel. I told a mechanic that some mornings the fuel gauge was reading almost empty when it had shown half-full when I parked up the night before.

'That's because your trucks are used at night for jobs around the site,' he told me. I asked who was driving them to be told it was some bulldozer and crane drivers getting a bit of overtime. I was not having this and went to the site boss along with John and Andy. The gaffer tried to wriggle out of it at first by saying that HGV drivers could only drive so many hours a day.

'That's bullshit,' I told him. 'The rules on hours don't apply if you're driving on a building site.'

In fact, you don't even need an HGV licence, or any sort of licence, to drive on private property. Over the next few weeks, the three of us were given as many shitty jobs as the boss could dream up but we never flinched. When we were not given a fair amount of overtime, we would take the lorry keys home or disable the truck one way or another. Finally, things came to a head.

I was checking the oil in my truck one morning when John MacKay came out of the gaffer's cabin.

'I've just been fired along with Andy,' he said.

In my view the sackings were unjustified and I marched into the gaffer's office to tell him so. He was sitting behind his desk with a smug look on his face and before I opened my mouth he shouted:

'Don't bother saying anything, Keeman, you're fired as well.' We got what wages were due and were escorted off the site. A visit to the Ministry of Labour in Bath Street was a waste of time; there were no Industrial Tribunals at the time and suing an employer was a very difficult process based on a breach of contract, so our only option was to look for another job. An opportunity came that afternoon when Andy learned that W H Malcolm in Paisley were looking for tipper drivers. He called them and an arrangement was made for the three of us to have an interview around seven that evening, at their Paisley Depot. We were interviewed at the same time by a guy whom I thought was an arrogant bastard and I knew I would never be able to work with him so I rose to leave.

'Where are you going?' he asked.

'As far away from you as possible,' I said, and walked out.

I waited outside for John and Andy and when they appeared, they had both been given a start and told me the guy said I could start along with them if I wanted, but I never did.

We made it back to the Two Ways bar in time for a couple of pints before it closed. I ordered the beers and when I took my cash from my pocket, I pulled out a bunch of keys.

'What's the keys for?' Andy asked. I had a look at them before answering.

'Looks like they're keys for a Bedford Tipper.'

Following a conversation with one of my old customers I learned that a coal merchant, W. J. Ritchie, was looking for drivers.

'But if you ever worked on the buses don't tell him,' he said. 'He hates bus drivers; he says they're lazy bastards too used to their loads walking on and off and the only thing they ever lift is their wages.'

Ritchie's had an office next to the Corporation Weighbridge in Minerva Street, and I called there early the next morning. Walter Ritchie, the company's owner, spoke with me about my driving experience which by that time was considerable. The Government had introduced HGV Licences in February 1970 and drivers who were qualified to drive lorries on their ordinary licence were required to undergo a medical costing two guineas and sit a driving test costing six pounds. If you could get a company to complete a form stating you had six month's experience as a lorry driver during the year 1969, you were exempt from the test, but not the medical. I had gained exemption through my time with Bilslands and was licensed to drive Class 2 HGVs, so I got a job. He told me he would ask for my National Insurance Card in a week or so if I performed well enough but it was weeks later before he did. Meanwhile, everything I earned was paid over with no deductions.

Ritchie's had a number of contracts with the Glasgow Corporation, among which was the job of stocking the coal cellars of libraries, schools, police offices and other public buildings during the summer. In one school on St George's Road, the janitor had a school blackboard in the cellar on which he'd written 'big pail' and 'wee pail'. Under each heading he had a five-bar gate method of counting the number of pails and I was intrigued so I asked among the drivers, but it was Walter Ritchie himself who provided the answer. He told me this was the janitor's way of checking that when the coal was delivered, he was getting a full ten-tons. Apparently, he knew roughly how many pounds of coal each pail held and when he carried a pail to the boiler, he ticked whether he'd used the big pail or the wee pail. Considering I used to deliver about forty tons over the course of a week it was months before he could confirm whether the correct amount had been delivered and by then nobody would have listened to him in any case.

Ritchie's also had tippers on hire to the roads department and I spent some time driving a squad of men around Glasgow with a couple of tons of tar in the back, along with a roller and other tools, looking for holes on the pavements and streets. I also spent time working on demolition with the Corporation's building department shifting the rubble from the demolished tenements, particularly in the East End, and a good knowledge of Glasgow's scrap yards was handy for this position. Along with small, Bedford ex-army tippers, Ritchie's also had some coal lorries, a couple of Scania articulated lorries and a six-wheel AEC Mandator. Of all the different types of job I did with Ritchie's, the most memorable was shifting sewage with a tipper at the Dalmuir Sewage Works. I arrived and a guy opened a large door and waved me back into the work area. There was a tiled pool of brown-coloured water, the walls and floors were tiled and the whole surrounding area was spotless. I reversed up to the edge of the pool and the JCB driver dipped his bucket into the water and when it broke a horrendous smell permeated all around. I felt physically sick. He loaded the buckets of sewage on to the back of my wagon and pointed to the nearby fields.

'Just let it run out evenly across the fields,' he said.

I spent the next six hours dumping this shit across the fields one load after another, the lorry was absolutely filthy at the end of my shift, but I was given access to a high-powered steam cleaner and soon it was gleaming.

'You only have to go through it for another week,' said the JCB driver.

'Try practicing breathing through your mouth tomorrow, it doesn't smell so bad that way.' I was grateful when that particular job came to an end.

There was a miner's strike in 1972 and after it was settled most of the coal from Northern pits was being taken south with few deliveries to Scotland. Walter agreed with the Corporation to send three tippers down to Seaton Burn pit, near Newcastle, in the middle of the night. Each would load ten tons of coal and deliver it to a Glasgow school or library later that day. I came up the A1 on the way back with my first load and just after eleven in the morning I stopped at the last pub in England, in Berwick and Tweed, for a sandwich and a soft drink. I parked in the hotel car park and when I entered the bar the barman asked me if I was the driver of the coal lorry. I thought he was about to complain about my parking in the car park so I asked him if there was a problem.

'Not at all,' he said. 'It's just been a while since we've been able to get any coal up here because of the strike.'

'I see,' I said, noticing that the large coal fire in the bar was burning wood, and producing more smoke than flame.

'I'll throw you off a few lumps for the fire if you like,' I offered, and he was out of the door like a shot with me following him. I climbed up on to the lorry and threw over as much coal as would have filled a couple of bags and he barrowed it to a coal bunker in the back garden. When I went back into the bar, he prepared some cheese toasties and a couple of bottles of orange juice. On the second day, when we were ready to leave the pit with our loads, one of the other drivers asked me why I went north via the A1 instead of going over the A68 to Longtown. I just shrugged and went on my way. I wasn't having him muscle in on my free lunches. This run lasted for about ten days when coal deliveries by rail got back to normal and we resumed our daily jobs back in Glasgow.

I was put on a run that meant driving to Dunoon early every morning, for two or three weeks, to deliver coal to an outdoor education centre for deprived children. Castle Toward was a country house overlooking Rothesay Bay on the west-coast of Scotland. Built in the 1800s, it replaced an earlier castle which was the ancestral home of the Lamont family. After the war it was sold to Glasgow Corporation and used as an outdoor education facility for children until its closure in 2014. My job was to stock it with coal until the bunkers were full which took about three weeks delivering ten tons each day. I loved that particular task as the drive round Loch Lomond in the early morning as the sun came up was truly beautiful.

After completing the Dunoon run, I was sent on hire to Barlinnie Prison. The young offenders there were put to work stripping the tin and wax paper covering from copper cables. A scrap-metal dealer collected the copper and we collected the rest and dumped it at the coup in Easterhouse.

The prisoners placed a table at the rear of the lorry and two of them lifted large sheets filled with this residue and handed them up to their colleagues who tipped the rubbish into the back of the tipper. As the driver I was required to remain in the cab whilst it was being loaded. It was a long process as the inmates were never in any hurry to load the truck and neither were the prison officers. A driver who had been on this run before me told me to take up a couple of packets of tobacco and drop them into the back of the truck. In return the inmates would include lumps of copper along with the rubbish. On my very first visit I followed his instructions: I opened the cab door, stood on the wing and looked in the back of the truck, dropping in the tobacco as I did so. Unfortunately, an officer on a balcony above spotted the manoeuvre and I was quickly in trouble. After pleading I was only trying to encourage the men to load a bit quicker, I was allowed to continue my shift. When I got back to the depot Walter told me that he had received a call from Barlinnie saying I was barred.

'I'll keep that in mind,' I said, 'if a judge ever tries to send me there.'

Two weeks later one of the prisoners escaped in the back of a lorry and my replacement driver was interrogated by the CID and the prison authorities for hours. He genuinely had no knowledge of the escape and the escapee was later arrested at his mother's house in Easterhouse.

After a number of weeks, Walter had still not made me a full-time employee and had not asked for my Insurance Cards. Following an argument one Friday evening he told me not to come back. In a way I was quite happy with this as I wanted some guarantee of full-time work and was getting into a bit of a rut. So, I told Janet when I got home that I was finished and intended to look for a full-time job the following Monday. On the Saturday morning I was in bed when Janet woke me to say someone was at the door. I looked through

80

the spyglass to see Walter's son, generally known as Young Walter, standing on the landing. I opened the door and before I could say anything young Walter blurted out:

'My dad said you've slept in for your work. You have two loads to deliver to the Central Police Office this morning.'

'Your dad told me not to come back last night so I'm finished. Tell him I'm fed up being fired one minute and restarted the next. I'm not coming in.'

Walter shrugged and I went downstairs and sat down with Janet to have some breakfast. I hadn't finished eating when Young Walter was back at the door:

'My dad said to tell you unless you do those two deliveries, he's going to park your pal's car at the traffic lights on Finnieston Street.'

This was a reference to my mate Alec who had asked me if I could park his Austin-7 somewhere free from the prying eyes of the police until he got it taxed and insured. I had asked Walter Sr. some weeks before if I could park the car in the yard and he'd agreed. I knew he was a man of his word; when he said he'd park Alec's car at the traffic lights, that's exactly what he'd do. When I went into the office for the truck keys, he laughed.

'Sleep in, did you?' I called him a blackmailing bastard and went to work.

Ritchie's business was expanding and he moved to larger premises on the London Road near Mount Vernon. It was a large yard which was formerly a steel works, but for me it was too far to travel every day. I worked from the new yard for a few weeks but after numerous arguments, chiefly over money and hours, I decided to leave. By this time, Alec had sorted his car tax and insurance and there was nothing to keep me.

Chapter Seven

Three Jobs in One Day

During the few weeks I was working at Ritchie's new depot I spoke with Janet's brother, Bruce, about a job at the coal depot on Crow Road where he worked. He spoke with one of the coal merchants who said he could use a driver and I should give him a phone. This call led to a new start immediately after I left Ritchie's. After a few weeks bagging coal from railway wagons and selling it round the houses in Partick, I was offered work on the tippers. With these you pulled a lever inside the cab and your load fell off. Selling coal from a truck meant you carried it on your back and there were some four-storey tenements in Partick. By the time you got to the top with a bag on your back your legs were shaking like an Elvis impersonator. Mr. Black, my new employer, had a few contracts with the Corporation and the drivers had to wait every morning until a job was phoned in. If no work turned up you didn't get paid. On one of these mornings, things were very quiet so I drove my tipper down to the workshop on South Street. I steam-cleaned the truck and gave the chassis, wheels and bumpers a coat of black paint. When I arrived back at the yard the boss was so impressed with my initiative that he suggested I should wash and paint the other tippers. When I pointed out that these were the responsibility of the other drivers who, incidentally, were sitting in a hut playing cards at the time, he asked me whether I wanted to work or not. My response left me unemployed yet again. However, it was only around ten in the morning so there was plenty time to have a cup of tea and look for another job.

Around eleven o'clock I paid a visit to Partick Labour Exchange. I was advised that a printing firm in Holdsworth Street was looking for a driver. Armed with my job card I went along and had an interview with the assistant manager. After about five minutes he told me I could have the job if I wanted it but I'd have to wait until his boss came back from lunch to tell me what the wages were. Meanwhile he suggested I could do a few local deliveries by which time the boss would be back. I agreed to this and after an hour or so returned to the depot to find that unfortunately the wage rate was well below what I had been earning and we could not agree a rate for the job. He paid me a couple of pounds for what I'd delivered and I was back at the Labour Exchange just after lunch. This time they sent me for an interview with John Young's chemical works in Elliot Street and by three in the afternoon I was sitting in a queue at King George V docks waiting for the dockers to unload ten tons of DDT, a black foul-smelling disinfectant, which is banned nowadays, for shipment to Africa. Young had two vehicles: a ten-ton flatbed lorry and a small pick-up truck. The pick-up was used for delivering five-gallon drums of disinfectant and other cleaning materials, to schools and other Corporation buildings and the flatbed for bulk deliveries to the docks in Glasgow for shipping overseas. The pick-up was driven by an older guy who spent most of the morning polishing it until the dispatch department decided on his deliveries for the day. Meanwhile I was busy running between the depot and the docks. When I suggested that perhaps we could take turns at driving the pick-up and the lorry I was told that Willie's eyes were bad and he had difficulty driving the larger vehicle, especially going round corners. This sounded reasonable enough until I found out that Willie actually earned more than me and, whereas I was lifting about thirty tons in weight every day, the heaviest thing Willie was lifting was his wages. When there were no deliveries for the docks,

I just hung around the factory making a nuisance of myself. Health and Safety was non-existent at this time and when I walked around the factory ten-gallon barrels of arsenic lay against walls without lids. There was enough arsenic on the premises to kill everyone in Glasgow.

The company employed carriers to deliver their products outside the Glasgow area and I got talking with a driver from British Road Services who was picking up deliveries for the Stirling/Perth/Dundee run. He seemed to have much better working conditions than I'd ever had in the haulage business and offered to speak for me if I applied to his depot in Lister Street. I did not know where that was but it turned out to be near the Venereal Disease Clinic in Black Street. As Billy Connolly put it - anyone going in the door wore a T-shirt with the words written on the back: 'Honest I'm a Joiner Working in Here.'

The BRS was the government's nationalised transport industry with depots in every city, town, village and hamlet in the UK. In terms of the trade union it was a closed shop so I joined the Transport and General Workers Union when I got the job. I really don't think I've ever worked with such a great bunch of guys in my life. They really believed that an attack on one was an attack on all, like some latter-day musketeers. Being on strike was as much part of the job as working and for the most part the workers ran the place. In my particular depot we had a communist shop steward for a while, and I often think we spent more time picketing the place than we did driving. The withdrawal of labour was called for the most pedantic reasons and a strike could last for a few minutes or a couple of days.

On reflection, Fridays were bad days for managers because workers were paid on Thursdays and no one felt like doing too much on a Friday, after spending the previous evening in the pub. However, there were also serious industrial disputes and in 1972 we were on strike for almost three months for an increase in wages. Our basic wage at the time was around eighteen pounds a week, but we earned more than that with bonuses, including things like tonnage money, London allowance and 'dark money'- extra cash for driving in the dark. However, when it came to holiday pay, we were paid the basic rate which did not help if you wanted to actually go on holiday. We went on strike for forty pounds for a forty-hour week. In terms of percentages this looks absurd nowadays being around one-hundred and twenty-two percent of an increase, but the arithmetic is correct.

In the beginning I was sent to work on a particular contract with the Irish section of the BRS known as Containerway. They had a main depot in Ardrossan, near the ferry terminal, but I was assigned to the depot in Balmore Road, Possilpark. Containerway delivered all sorts of products produced in Ireland to factories, shops and other businesses on mainland Britain. They also had a contract with Hoover of Cambuslang to deliver vacuum cleaners, washing machines and other white goods across Northern Ireland. This part of the UK was in turmoil in the 1970s and as drivers we were advised to keep our mouths shut about the situation while in the country and refrain from passing any personal opinions. After doing our daily deliveries we drove to digs in Larne every night which was thought to be pretty free from much trouble. I never told Janet when I was on the Irish run, saying I was driving in the North of England.

When I really was on the Newcastle run, I stayed each night at the YMCA in North Shields which had a dormitory for long-distance drivers. We paid for the digs but they were reasonably cheap and I suppose helped the organisation help others. I drank in a local bar filled with shipyard workers from Swan Hunter's yard. My father, being a shipyard worker himself, meant I got on well with the locals and Glaswegians of that era had a great deal in common with Geordies. Around that time Swan Hunter was building a large tanker, with engines built by John Brown's yard at Clydebank. It was launched as 'Texaco Great Britain', in March 1971. I was in the bar in North Shields the week before the launch when the shipyard workers were talking about the ship. It was over thirteen-hundred feet long and to me it looked like the Tyne wasn't that wide. I asked some of the guys in the pub what would happen if they couldn't get it turned in time and with typical northern humour the reply came back:

'We'll have another bridge across the Tyne.'

As it was, the launch was perfect: four tugs pushed her round and she sat proudly in the middle of the river. Sadly, in 1976, eight workers were killed in an explosion at the yard.

I was earning quite good money with the BRS and we had a lot of friends we met up with at weekends. On Saturday mornings I played snooker at the Royal Artillery Club in Elmbank Crescent with the Gilmour brothers, Willie Middleton-Middy and David Gilfillan. We'd go into Pat Orr's bookmakers on Kent Road and lay some bets on the horseracing and football for the day, before getting to the club for opening time. One Saturday morning I suggested to Pat that we could leave some money with him and phone our bets through later, as we were having a few non-runners because our bets were normally on very early. He agreed and we worked that way for a couple of weeks. Very quickly the word went round that we could get a bet on just before the 'off' and we were approached by other club members. After the first few bets were taken, I suggested that we didn't phone them through to Pat but laid them ourselves. We could pool our money and pay out on the winners. If any of the bets were too much for us to lay, we would phone them to Pat. This went down well and for about four weeks we made a profit. On our last Saturday as bookies I was handling the bets when Middy laid a bet.

'Who's it for?' I asked.

'Me,' he said.

Then he went on to explain he was fed up and preferred to back his own horses. Despite my pointing out that we had made a profit every week he was not for moving so we went back to losing. Gamblers? They have no logic at times. Meanwhile, I had a word with Pat about taking bets from other members and asked for some commission which he agreed to pay so we got something out of it.

We went to a number of military clubs in those days including the Cameron Highlanders at Queen's Crescent, near St George's Cross, the HLI club, and RAFA in Ashley Street, near Charing Cross. At these clubs the drink was cheap; you could play bingo, dance and join in the singing, usually accompanied by a dodgy piano player. They were very similar to the Working Men's clubs I'd visited in the North of England.

On some Saturday evenings, particularly if we had won on the afternoon horse-racing, we would go to Shawfield Greyhound Stadium. One time we had been in the Royal Artillery Club most of the day when Middy suggested we go to the dogs. I rejected the idea, as I had arranged to take Janet out, and left the club early. Janet and I went for a meal and a few drinks and were home just after midnight. Early on the Sunday morning there was a knock at the door and when I opened it, Middy was standing there clearly the worse for wear.

'I'm just out of the jail,' he said and went on to explain. He, along with Bobby Gilmour and David Gilfillan, had left the Royal Artillery Club around seven. Bobby, who worked with Whatlings, had a work's van and drove the other two to the Politician pub on Maryhill Road, across the road from where he stayed in the Wynford Estate. He parked the van outside his flat and went to the pub with Middy and David. Some hours later they were still there when Middy asked Bobby to drive him and David to Shawfield. Bobby, recognising he was too drunk to drive, refused, but in a moment of madness, handed over the keys of the van and went home. Middy and David then decided to drive themselves to the dogs and, although neither of them had a licence, they were doing okay until they reached Renfield Street where they hit three parked cars. Shawfield was now off the agenda and their next barmy idea was to drive to my house in Kent Road and ask me for help. Of course, Janet and I were out for the evening so they proceeded to drive on, intending to go to David's house in Partick. When they got to the bottom of Kent Road, where it meets Argyle Street, David, who was having a go at the driving following Middy's collisions, turned sharp right taking him west on Argyle Street on the wrong side of the road. With traffic approaching directly in front of him he panicked, mounted the pavement and hit the building that housed the Berkeley Pub. Soon after the police carted them both off to the pokey.

After Middy explained this sequence of events, he asked what he should do. I told them if he mentioned that Bobby had given him the keys to the van, Whatlings would most likely fire him. I suggested it would be better if he said that he lifted the keys from the pub table or something along those lines. As David was driving when the police arrived, he would be the one charged with drunk driving. I suggested to Middy that he started to save up for a hefty fine and consider the possibility of some jail time. We then went to see David and Bobby and sorted out how to distribute the blame as fairly as possible. In the end Bobby kept his job.

On the day of Middy's trial, I received a message when I arrived at the depot at the end of my shift. It was from Middy and it asked if I would phone him at the Two Ways pub. I knew instantly that the trial was over and he hadn't been sent to jail at least. Anxious to know what the outcome was, I phoned from the traffic office. He was obviously full of good cheer and invited me to come for a drink as he had 'plenty of money.' He had saved up over a hundred pounds but was only fined twenty. I was being fined more than that for not filling in a log book. I later relieved him of some of the cash for my 'advice.' It was a good time to be young as long as you had work, but, as has been said, 'they are not long the days of wine and roses.'

Coming up for my fifth year with the BRS, rumours began to circulate that the Government had plans to make major changes. In the event the company was split up into different areas of the country and renamed Eastern, Western, Southern, Scottish and so on. Later it would be sold into private hands with a worker's shareholding. With Scottish Road Services, who were now my new employers, overtime was cut as were certain working practices. Formerly with BRS if you were going to England you could leave on a Sunday with double time and an overnight stay somewhere on your journey. This practice was abolished with much protest.

To subsidise my wages, I worked with my brother-in-law Bruce, who had persuaded his coal merchant boss that if he loaned us a truck, we could sell a couple of tons of his coal at the weekend. On Saturday mornings we went 'hawking' coal round Partick and Possilpark. We finished up in the Rosevale bar in the afternoon, black as the ace of spades and drinking McEwan's beer laced with a sprinkling of coal dust - a state of affairs that continued until the expected voluntary redundancies in the BRS were announced. I volunteered, but my application was rejected. I was unhappy with this decision as it was clear my family would soon have to move to another area as our tenement building in Kent Road was due for demolition. In fact, we soon had an offer of a house in Fort William that we rejected but accepted the offer of a house in Irvine on the Ayrshire coast.

My employers stuck to their guns saying there was a job for me and I was sent to an interview with the BRS Parcels Division in Warroch Street. Sometimes you need a bit of luck in life and I had it that day when I found out the manager of the Argyll Group was a former shop steward who had jumped ship. During the course of the interview I reminded him how easy it was within the BRS for a reluctant employee to cause industrial unrest. The company's trucks hadn't been replaced in years and it was a poor driver who could not find a reason for refusing to take a specific lorry on the road. Drivers carried a form that entitled them to draw cash from any other BRS depot and to request mechanical repairs. On one occasion I was driving a lorry that had a gear-oil leak seeping over one of the back wheels. Every two weeks when my truck had a service I wrote on the form: 'Oil leak nearside rear wheel,' but it was never repaired. I got fed up with this and submitted a form which said: 'Oil leak seeping from half shaft over nearside rear wheel. Please replace half-shaft seals and top-up differential with gear oil.' According to the senior mechanic this was interpreted as my telling his mechanics how to do their job and they refused to work on my lorry until I apologised. I went to a meeting with my shop steward, my manager and the chief mechanic and his manager. I apologised and agreed I was not a qualified mechanic and they agreed to service the truck and sort the oil leak. Shortly afterwards I put five trucks off the road, all of which had defects that could have resulted in my being booked by the police. On each form I simply wrote, 'Motor broke.' They got the message and I never had any more trouble from the workshop.

My prospective new manager was aware of this incident and the fact that I once asked for a vote of no confidence in a shop steward, when he'd unilaterally agreed with the manager that drivers whose trucks were under repair or in for a service would sweep up around the depot. When my manager asked me to do so I told him I didn't hold an HGV Licence for brushing floors and he sent me home. I formed a picket line at the gate and when drivers started arriving, I explained what my manager and shop steward had agreed.

My view was this agreement constituted a unilateral change to my terms and conditions and consequently was illegal. The drivers agreed, voted no confidence in the steward, and I was eventually paid for the wages I'd lost.

At the meeting with the manager of the Parcels Division I told him I was offered a new house too far from work to travel every day. On reflection, he advised the management team it was probably in the best interests of the business to let me go. Within a few weeks I was on my way to our new home in Irvine with my redundancy pay in my pocket and confident I would get a new job. This confidence, as it turned out, was somewhat misplaced.

Royal Artillery Club Glasgow 1960s

Chapter Eight

Moving House

I was 31, Janet, 29, John, 7 and James, 5. Janet was expecting our third child despite having been told by doctors she could not have any more children after James was born in 1970. We arrived on a Saturday afternoon with our furniture in the back of a Scottish Road Services truck driven by my old pal from the Glasgow Hiring Company, John MacGonagle, who had defected to the Scottish Road Services. The last thing left in the Kent Road house before we moved was a piano. I asked John what we should do with it and he quietly pulled the room door closed. After we had emptied the truck into our new home I travelled back to Glasgow with John, Middy and David to buy them a drink as they wouldn't accept any payment for doing the removal. Janet settled into sorting out what she could and we agreed we had the rest of our lives to get the house in shape so we would start the heavy stuff the following day. By the Sunday evening we had most of the house cleaned, beds and wardrobes assembled, rooms allocated, the children bathed and the television working. We both had a bath before we went to bed. For the first time in both our lives we were living in a house with a bathroom.

We did not make a good start to life in our new home. Within weeks of moving in Janet had to go back to Glasgow to be admitted to the Queen Mother's Hospital as her pregnancy was at risk. After weeks in hospital being monitored, she had to have an emergency Caesarean, but gave birth to a healthy boy we named Stephen. He was born on the 2nd of December 1975. Janet made it home in time for Christmas, but she haemorrhaged and was rushed to Ayrshire Central Hospital where it was concluded that part of the placenta had been left inside after the Caesarean operation. She recovered from this setback but had to have an operation to prevent any further pregnancies at Ballochmyle Hospital in Mauchline. But she was not finished with hospitals yet.

One Saturday evening her mother came down from Glasgow to watch the boys and let us have our first night out in months. We got dressed up and went over to a local pub for a drink before setting off for a meal. Janet was sitting on a bar stool as I ordered the drinks when suddenly she felt faint and fell to the ground, banging her head. I got her home and called a doctor who had her admitted to Kilmarnock Hospital. Following an examination and X-ray, it was discovered she had fractured her skull.

Not long after this, when she was fully recovered, we experienced another drama. We were watching BBC's Midnight Movie on a Saturday night when we heard noises coming from the house next door. It was a cracking noise and when I opened the front door, I saw flames coming from my neighbour's window. The next thing I saw was my neighbour jumping over the window into the gardens below. I raised the alarm along the corridor and we got the children out of their beds and into the street out of harm's way. Billy, our neighbour, broke some bones in his hand when he jumped but he was otherwise okay and no one else was hurt. To add to these problems, I was having difficulty getting work as a driver. I was getting unemployment benefit with an additional Earning's Related Supplement, which was calculated on your previous earnings; the more you earned, the higher the rate. In fact, most of the driving jobs available paid less than I was getting in benefits, but this benefit would not be paid indefinitely. I needed work, but the jobs I was offered were mostly short term or part time. One that was really short was an interesting four days working in a beer tent at the Open Golf Championship in Troon in 1982 when Tom Watson won the title. On the Sunday me and a guy I'd met picked up what we were owed, and went to watch the golf. Over the four days we'd met lots of staff from other hospitality tents and we joined them for a picnic. We had smoked salmon, champagne, an assortment of wine and spirits, and loads of beer, free gratis.

I followed Watson for a couple of holes and was right behind him as he teed off at one hole. We could clearly hear his caddy tell him it was a dog leg to the left but if he aimed it to the right the wind would guide it left round the dog leg. He took a couple of practice swings, hit the ball, and it travelled to the right looking like it was headed into the sea. Just before it reached the water it began to turn left as the wind caught it and ended up in the middle of the fairway. Wow!

Meanwhile my other neighbour, an engineer with ICI at Ardeer in Stevenston, got me an application form for a job with his employers on a production line making detonators. I applied and was accepted following an interview. Every morning when I arrived at work I was required to change out of my clothes and dress in a lamb's wool jersey and trousers and rubber shoes. All jewellery, watches, bracelets, and money were locked in a locker and you went down a tunnel into the area where the detonators were made. All these precautions were to avoid causing a spark and consequently an explosion. Training involved learning the different stages in the manufacturing of detonators.

A monkey of average intelligence could have learned the process in a few hours, but I was advised I would spend a week on each stage. One process involved putting your right foot on a pedal and turning a wheel on a wall until you felt a certain amount of pressure at which point you pushed the pedal with your foot to the floor. The skill required for this job had been automated when some bright spark decided to paint a mark on the wheel and one on the wall, so when the two marks matched up, that was the signal to push the pedal.

Every now and again someone would fail to follow the process correctly and a minor explosion would occur. On these occasions we were allowed a ten-minute smoke break to recover from the shock, before we went back down the hole again. During the summer, when the factory closed down for two weeks, I was asked if I wanted to work with some of the maintenance guys as I had no holiday pay due, so I went to work with the tinsmiths. This was a reasonably interesting job but when I applied, I was told that such vacancies were filled according to length of service one had with the company. I reckoned that on these criteria I had about thirty years to do before I could get out of the detonator department.

I began to feel unwell and lost some time off work on a regular basis. I had no idea what was wrong with me but eventually Janet encouraged me to see a doctor. He diagnosed I was suffering from depression and prescribed some tablets, but they did not help. I finally gave up my job and spent a lot of time in bed. I lost weight and had fits of crying for no apparent reason. Janet went to see my doctor and told him about my behaviour and a few hours later he had me admitted to Ailsa Hospital on the outskirts of Ayr. I knew nothing about mental illness or depression. I merely concluded I was going mad and when I entered the hospital, I believed this was where I would spend the rest of my life. I was treated with tablets and when little progress was made, they tried hypnotherapy, but that did not improve my condition either. I was allowed home some weekends but I just went to bed for most of the time before returning to hospital on Sunday evenings.

After some months it was decided to try a treatment known as Electro Convulsive Therapy, commonly referred to as Electric Shock Treatment. Janet was advised it was better not to visit immediately after I'd had a treatment as she would see a vast improvement that suggested I was back to normal, but it would be short lived. I received over a dozen of these treatments and slowly but surely, I began to regain some of my confidence and the depressive thoughts, bouts of crying and suicidal tendencies began to disappear. After over three months in hospital I was discharged and put on medication with monthly visits to a psychiatrist.

I began to think of going back to work and applied for a number of jobs without success until I saw an advert for a driving vacancy with a local carrier. I applied and was given an interview, but I didn't tell Janet until I was actually offered and accepted the job. When I told her, I expected her to be very happy I was going back to work and getting out from under her feet, but she did not look at all pleased. I pressed her as to why and she finally told me that my psychiatrist had told her that I would really not manage to go back to driving vehicles. He reckoned my nerves would not stand up to it and she should try and discourage me from applying for that sort of job and I should try something less stressful like gardening. I had the greatest respect for this doctor, who had worked tirelessly to get me well, but on this occasion, I felt he was wrong. I told Janet I felt I had to go back to work and promised if I felt I could not handle it I would give it up.

The following Monday I reported for duty to John Fraser and Sons, Quarry Road, Irvine. It had been almost two years since I'd driven a truck and I was a bit rusty but after a drive up to Glasgow, I was back in the groove and felt better than I had in two years. I got the work done without difficulty that first day. Fraser's picked up cheese, butter and other foodstuffs, along with fruit and vegetables from the Glasgow Fruit Market and delivered them around Irvine and the west coast as far as Dumfries and Stranraer. I settled in and was coping okay but still seeing my psychiatrist once a month. After six months or so I attended my monthly meeting. As usual he asked me how I was coping with the job and he was quite delighted with my responses.

'There's something I want to say but I don't know how to go about it,' I said.

'Just say it in your own words, John,' he said.

'I don't want to appear ungrateful, doctor,' I said, 'but I don't feel I need to come here anymore.'

He looked thoughtful before he responded.

'Well John,' he said. 'I've waited a long time to hear you say that and I'm very happy you have. Now I'll arrange for your prescriptions to be managed by your GP.'

It was then I told him I had stopped taking the pills some three weeks before.

'And how have you managed?' He asked.

I explained that I was a bit worried at first but everything was back to normal and I felt I did not need that sort of support anymore. So, we parted and I went back to work.

About two weeks later I saw him getting out of his car in Ayr. I pulled into the side of the road behind him and when I slammed on the air brakes of the truck he flinched at the hissing noise. I jumped down from the truck:

'How's the nerves, Doc?' I asked.

He took one look at me, looked up at the truck and shook his head.

'You know something John, I never really thought you would make a full recovery like this. I am so happy for you and your family.'

I swear I saw the makings of a tear in his eye. With that doctor's help and the help from my GP and the staff at Ailsa Hospital I had recovered from a very debilitating mental illness. It took a long time but all through that time the one person who never wavered, who never thought of giving up, and who was always by my side was my dear wife, Janet. Where she got the energy to look after the three boys, run the house and visit me regularly at the hospital I'll never know. She is the most loving person I have ever met in my whole life.

The drivers at Frasers were good workmates. Some of them had been with the firm for a few years but I and another Glasgow man had a lot less service. Things were going quite well until one Christmas Eve. George Fraser, the son of the man who had started the business many years before, gave all the staff a cash bonus, a tin of biscuits and a card for their partners, and then took us for a Chinese meal. During the meal he gave me and Billy a week's notice as the company was 'struggling financially.' So, on New Year's Eve I was unemployed again but with an assurance that if things picked up, I would get started back.

Early in the New Year our former boss had managed to obtain the cash to purchase three new wagons after negotiating a contract with an Irvine company and we were both called back to work. The new contract involved delivering ladies nightdresses from Irvine to London and South Wales on a weekly basis. As I had been on long distance work with the BRS years before, he asked if I would get the job up and running for the first month or so then he would put the drivers on a rota. I agreed and as I set off for my first run to London, I felt happier than I had in years.

If there's anything a person needs to get through this world it's confidence and through my runs to London and Wales, I knew I was back to my old self. Janet must have felt that as well as she never flinched when I took the two older boys with me. I could not take them both together. I wasn't that confident. On one trip to London with James we were walking along the Thames Embankment looking at the boats that plied their trade with cruises on the river. James wanted to go on a cruise but we were due to stay another night in Wales and I was a bit short of cash. The cruise he picked included a basket meal but I asked the guy if I could just pay for the trip without the evening meal, explaining I was a driver and a bit short of cash.

'I can do that,' he said, 'and I won't charge for the kid.' The look on my son's face when I said we could go was priceless. About half-way through the cruise a girl came round with the chicken-in-a-basket and handed it to James.

'You've to share that with your dad,' she said.

I never forgot these simple gestures that made my son so happy that evening. On another trip, this time with John, we were staying in Towyn, a seaside resort in North Wales. After I parked the truck for the night, we were walking along the sea-front when I thought I saw a camel on a grassy patch between two buildings. I thought it was perhaps time I went to bed but we crossed over the road anyway to satisfy my curiosity. Sure as eggs are egg-shaped, it was indeed a camel; there was also an elephant and some other exotic animals, a Llama for one. They belonged to a circus that was being set up in the fields behind the buildings on the sea-front and these animals were chained to the ground but due to the long grass you couldn't see they were tethered. A few days later we were in Torquay and went to the theatre to see Russ Abbot. He started the show by reading out a seat number and telling the occupant they had won a moped. It turned out to be a mop head. John laughed all the way through the show.

A typical week would begin by leaving Irvine on a Sunday afternoon and driving to Morecambe, staying overnight at the Marsdene Guest House in Townley Street, after a few beers on the Pier. After breakfast on Monday morning I'd make my way to Cardiff via the M6 and west along the A40. After delivering in Cardiff, I'd head back east staying at the Crown Hotel in Monmouth or Symonds Yat off the A40. They were good times.

One Monday night I was having a drink in the Crown with some locals watching the TV News. The small group around the television were particularly interested in an item about Operation Countryman, an investigation into corruption within Scotland Yard during the late 1970s. I piped up that I didn't see what the problem was, as London had always had

99

the best policemen that money could buy. The owner behind the bar advised me to watch what I was saying. I looked at him and saw the glint in his eye.

'You weren't, were you?' I asked.

'Twenty odd years with the Flying Squad,' he said.

I looked around the pub and turned back to him.

'So, this place is your pension eh? No wonder you can swan off to the French racing every other Sunday.'

He laughed and set up a free drink for the eight or nine of us at the bar. Apparently, he and his wife had won a few quid at Longchamp the day before.

As well as trips south, George Fraser managed to secure a contract to deliver machine parts to an oil-rig yard on the island of Stornoway. With three new vehicles he needed two drivers and I suggested two of my neighbours - the engineer John Fraser, who had initially got me a job in the ICI, and a guy from Glasgow called Jimmy Daley. They were both engaged and things went along quite nicely. The three of us used to go swimming on Saturday mornings at the Magnum Leisure Centre, but one morning John was on his way home from England so Jimmy and I went ourselves. We were swimming around when we noticed a fully dressed guy walking around the pool with what looked like a microphone and some recording equipment. He waved us over and when we came out of the pool he asked if we could do him a favour. He explained he was recording for a sound effects company and wanted us to dive into the pool together while he recorded the splash. After a few goes he was happy with the result and we returned to our swim. For months later when I saw a film that showed dolphins or sharks jumping in and out of the water I used to wonder if the noise of the splash was me and Jimmy.

With the new oil-rig contract in place, I travelled up one Saturday afternoon to Stornoway to deliver some urgently needed machine parts. I got the ferry over to the island and arrived around nine-thirty in the evening. The yard was open twenty-four hours a day so I delivered the parts when I disembarked. After the delivery I parked up on the pier and went to my digs in the town.

I was staying in a small bed and breakfast hotel run by the owners. After I came in from the local pub on Saturday night the owner's wife was peeling potatoes and preparing the Sunday dinner. I asked her why she was doing this so late at night and she said she did not work on the Lord's Day. She asked me if I was going to church on Sunday and I said if I did it would most likely fall down.

'We will be going in the morning and I would appreciate it if you did not turn the television on, we do not watch television on the Lord's day,' she said.

I nodded and said I would just read the Sunday newspapers, which she then told me did not arrive on the island until Monday morning. When Sunday morning arrived, I slept late and went out for a walk just after noon. It was a ghost town. Everything except the church was closed so I began to walk outside the town in the direction of the oil-rig yard. I remembered that they had a large canteen and I knew they worked on Sundays so I expected I could get a meal and perhaps a drink. On the way there I saw two men approach who clearly had been drinking. I stopped them and asked where they got the drink and they told me at the yard's social club but it only opened for an hour on a Sunday and had special permission from the local authority to do so. I asked what time they closed and was told one o'clock I looked at my watch and it was five-past. With no ferry sailings on a Sunday I was marooned on the island and spent most of the day wandering around counting sheep.

Not long after I returned to the mainland, I was in the polis's bad books. I was due to appear at Ayr Sheriff Court to answer a charge of speeding with a lorry on the Ayr Bypass. Speeding and log-sheet offences were hazards of the job and it was no big deal. I decided not to appear and sent in a letter pleading guilty. I mitigated my guilt by saying that my truck had recently been fitted with a tachograph that showed both miles and kilometres per hour and I mistook fifty miles per hour as fifty kilometres per hour. I happened to be through in Ayr on the day of my case so I went into the public gallery of the court to have a listen. After about an hour the Procurator Fiscal read out my charge and indicated I had sent in a letter with a mitigation plea.

'Oh, I suppose I must hear it,' the Sheriff said irritably. The clerk read out my excuse and the Sheriff sat shaking his head all the way through in utter disgust. When the clerk finished the Sheriff asked what speed I'd been doing. The clerk advised him it was fifty-eight in a forty limit.

'So, the difference was eighteen miles per hour. I impose a fine of one pound for each mile over the limit, and an endorsement on his licence.'

A couple of years later Fraser and Son was in financial difficulties and sold out to another company who offered workers a reduction in wages and extra hours, so I and another couple of drivers resigned. I fell out with my union, sued for constructive dismissal at an Industrial Tribunal and lost on a technicality.

I signed on at the local Job Centre and a clerk suggested I consider upgrading my Heavy Goods Vehicle Licence to a class that also covered articulated vehicles. I was also told that a Government Department, 'The Manpower Services Commission,' had a budget to fund HGV training for suitable applicants. I agreed to go for the training and the clerk filled in an application form on my behalf. Sometime later I was asked to attend an interview. On my arrival at the HGV Driving Test Centre in Prestwick, I was shown into an office and told I wasn't suitable for the training. The reason given was the speeding endorsement on my licence. I told him I had been waiting months for this course and nobody had mentioned this before. Then I asked him if the rule applied to those who were paying their own training fees. After some reluctance to answer he said it didn't. I raised a complaint with the Job Centre and their initial response was to say that I had not produced my licences at the Job Centre interview. I disputed their version of the event and asked to see the form. It was quite simple. If the form had my licence numbers in situ, then how did they get there? The reply was quite astonishing as they declared the form a classified government document. I contacted my MP, David Lambie, who offered his support. But despite his intervention, the form was not released. I received a letter saying the manager of the Job Centre wanted to call at my home to discuss the matter. I asked him more than once to produce the form but he stuck to his guns so I told him to leave before I threw him out. I then contacted a lawyer who laughed when I told him my application form was declared a classified government document. He called the Job Centre, spoke with the manager and gave him ten days to produce the form or he would apply for a court order. Three days later a copy of the form dropped through my door and it clearly showed my HGV and car licence numbers. In a pathetic attempt to cover up their incompetence someone had written above the column referring to driving licences: 'Licences not produced at interview.' I pointed this out to my MP and he was flabbergasted at the steps they had taken to protect themselves.

The Commission had the task of helping to alleviate the high levels of unemployment in the 1980s but being a Tory initiative it was doomed to fail, which it did. I hope I contributed to that failure in some very small way.

Full-time work was proving harder to get under yet another Tory, the well-loved Mrs Thatcher. I managed to get a number of part-time jobs including, among other things, driving taxis, ice cream vans and working with the mechanic who used to repair Fraser's trucks. He ran a small car-repair business in Irvine and I would do a bit of labouring when he needed help. It was a bit hit and miss though and one day I was using a grinder on a truck chassis when I got pieces of metal in one of my eyes. I went to the local chemist who took a look and phoned my doctor.

'Get to your GP right now,' she said.

I arrived at the surgery a few minutes later and the doctor put some drops in my eye and told me take a seat in the waiting room. Within a few seconds the pain was gone. 'Marvellous stuff,' I thought. That marvellous stuff turned out to be a local anaesthetic that froze my eye, and the doctor proceeded to remove small pieces of metal with a pair of tweezers whilst I sat frozen with fear and staring at the corner of the ceiling. Unfortunately, I had to go through the same process a few days later when my eye was very painful. What the doctor thought was a small indentation on my eyeball on first examination, caused by being hit with metal fragments, was in fact more metal filings that had to be removed.

I continued working part-time when I could and after a while, I got a job writing local community news with the *Irvine Times* and the *Irvine Herald*. It was all pretty basic stuff, finding out what was happening in terms of church socials, community council meetings, pub league football scores, school prize givings, charity events, and so on. One particular story caused a bit of embarrassment on my part and emphasises the old adage that you should never believe everything you read in a newspaper. I was told by Miss Smart, the head teacher at the local primary school, that the kids were organising a Burns Supper for senior citizens in the area. She told me a piper from the Dreghorn Pipe Band would pipe in the haggis and two of the children, a boy and a girl, would give the address to the lassies and to the haggis. The event was to take place on the following Tuesday evening. My weekly contribution to the newspaper was due to be handed in each Tuesday afternoon. If I left the story to the following week, I would not have been paid for it for another month, so I just wrote it up in the afternoon and handed it in. When I went round to see Miss Smart the following Thursday, she commented on the story. She said it was very interesting to read that everyone had a nice evening and the children did very well with their readings, but unfortunately, the actual event did not take place.

'If you remember,' she said, 'we had a heavy fall of snow late on Tuesday afternoon so we cancelled as we did not want the elderly put at risk of falls.'

Oh dear! I don't know why I bothered about when I'd be paid for the piece as the Social Security took most of the money I earned as I was on benefits so it was hardly worthwhile working at all. I was almost resigned to being on benefits until I was of pensionable age so I decided to sit the Higher English exam as a mature student at a local school - more as a personal challenge than anything else.

Following an interview with the Assistant Headmaster at Ravenspark Academy in Irvine, he agreed to put me forward as an external candidate. I wanted to sit the exam that was due in a few weeks and he advised me that I would fail and then I could come back to school the next term and 'do it properly.' I told him I had been reading and writing for over thirty years and didn't see any reason why I should fail. The only concern I had, having gone through some past exam papers, was the poetry section, so I asked if I could sit in on a class that was studying practical criticism of poetry and he arranged this.

During one of the classes we were reading a poem by Norman MacCaig entitled *Brooklyn Cop*. I was asked to interpret some parts of the poem to see if I understood it. When I said it was about a black New York policeman preparing to go to work at night in a violent society and wondering if he'd get safely home, I was interrupted by the teacher:

105

'He's not a black policeman,' she said. 'Where do you get the idea that he's black from?'

I thought for a minute and replied: 'The poet uses the term *steak-coloured*'.

'The policeman is white. Steak is red. The poet is describing a white, red-faced person,' she said, as if I didn't know what a steak looked like.

'It isn't red after you cook it and I still think he's black,' I ventured.

This brought howls of laughter from the class.

'Did you read the notes I gave you?' she asked and I replied in the affirmative.

'What did you think of them?' she continued.

'To be honest I think if the poet had actually thought of everything contained in the notes, he would have written a much better poem.'

This brought more laughter and, in the end, we agreed to disagree and I attended another two poetry classes.

I thought the young pupils were very laid back, to the point of couldn't care less. I met some of the boys one night in the Crown Hotel in Irvine. They were playing pool and when I said I wanted a game they asked me if I knew how to play. After I beat each of them one after another, they found out I did. I asked one of them if he had a play in mind for the English exam. Quick as a flash he told me *Romeo and Juliet* and added 'I haven't read it but I saw the film.' I often wonder how he got on with that tactic.

Soon after I sat the exam, I found out I could get financial support to go to college to study for Higher and Ordinary Grades on a full-time basis. I applied to Kilmarnock College and sat a further three Higher and two O-Grade examinations after a year. It was an interesting period being back at school aged forty. I'm not so sure that all the lecturers took kindly to teaching people older than themselves and, in many cases, with much more experience of the world of work than they had. My Modern Studies lecturer, Peter, was not one of them and seemed to relish the debates with the older students. One Friday morning he was going on at length about the Israeli and Palestine conflicts and during a short break one of the other students, a former British paratrooper, about ages with myself, asked me if I could come up with something that would slow Peter down a bit. I told him he was a bit behind with the syllabus and was trying to ensure he had covered everything before we sat the exams, hence the rate he was going at.

'I tell you what,' I said. 'Peter prides himself on his impartiality. He's standing for Parliament as a Liberal at the next election. When we go back after the break and he starts on about the Six Day War again, you stick your hand up and accuse him of being Pro-Israeli. He'll look for support and probably ask me what I think. I'll tell him I agree with you and we'll take it from there.'

We returned to the lecture theatre and Peter immediately launched into the issues surrounding the Six Day War. Suddenly the paratrooper piped up.

'Not the Jews again,' he said. 'Do the Palestinians not have a case to make? You've been going on about the Jews all morning as if the Arabs have no legitimate claim to anything.'

Peter looked a bit shell-shocked and glanced over at me. 'What do you think, John? Willie is suggesting I am being less than impartial in my lecture this morning. What's your opinion?'

I was desperately trying not to laugh, as was Willie who was sat at the far end of the room. Finally, I got it out:

'I think he has a point,' I said. 'If you take a look at my notes here, I have written nothing about the Palestinians.'

Peter stormed out of the room and we burst out laughing. He must have been away for about thirty minutes before he returned clutching a pile of books, followed by the librarian who was similarly laden. They both laid the books out on a table in front of the blackboard. Peter turned to me and Willie.

'Every one of these books was written by a Palestinian,' he said. 'They outline their case better than I ever could. I suggest you take a couple home and read them. I was intending to cover this later in my lecture and I will not be accused of being partial to any side.'

He looked at Willie who was smiling from ear to ear and then at me and I was similarly disposed. Then the penny dropped.

'You pair of bastards!' he said. 'If I was going on a bit you should have said.'

He was a lovely person and would have made a fine MP but the area he stood for would have voted for a monkey if it wore a Labour Party jersey.

On another day we got into an argument about rock and roll music when Peter said he would not allow one of his children to listen to a David Bowie record. I challenged him that this wasn't a very liberal approach and asked if he would have put up with his dad forbidding his music. He said something about music in his day being free from sexual innuendo and I burst out laughing.

'So, what was Little Richard singing about with his "Well Long Tall Sally is built for speed, she got everything that Uncle John need …"?' I asked.

What followed was a debate about modern music which was not part of the curriculum.

Economics was another subject where we found some humour. Our lecturer was a very smart dresser and well qualified in the subject but seemed to speak more about the music he liked, Frank Sinatra in particular, as well as Johnnie Walker whisky, and aeroplanes. In fact, it was rumoured that he was building his own light aircraft in a garage at his home. Just before we broke for the Christmas holidays, he gave us a question on economics to research over the holiday period.

He was at pains to ensure us that the test marks would not form part of our final marks, but was simply a test to see how we were progressing. We returned after the holidays and he collected our answers and told us to take a break for thirty minutes while he had a look through what we'd written. After he returned, he was handing our papers back when he stopped in front of Charlie Watt's desk.

'How did you find the test Mr Watt?' he asked.

'It was dead easy,' Charlie replied.

'I could tell that by the mark I gave you,' the lecturer said.

Of course, this remark raised a level of interest across the room.

'What did you get Charlie? What did you get?' some students were asking.

'Nothing!' said Charlie.

'Nothing!' I chimed in with my pennyworth. 'How could he have got no marks at all?' I asked.

The lecturer looked at Charlie. 'Do you want to read out your answer Mr Watt? You do not have to if you'd rather not.'

'That's okay,' said Charlie, as gallus as ever.

The following is a verbatim account of what he read that I have remembered for over thirty years.

Charlie began: 'As Frank Sinatra said, when he alighted from a Boeing 747 at Heathrow airport, clutching a glass of Johnnie Walker Black Label: the British economy is in a hell of a state.'

That was his complete answer. We gave him one mark as he had mentioned the word 'economy.'

I was grant funded for this course and because some of my subjects clashed, I had to study Higher History at a night class. Highers at school only counted as an O-Grade for grant purposes so I had to do another one to make up the necessary points for the grant. The only subject that fitted in with my others was Anatomy, Physiology and Health. I was in a class with one other male and eighteen females and became the subject of mirth during a lecture on blood cells. The lecturer asked if anyone would agree to have some blood taken so that the students could view it through a microscope and count the ratio of red-to-white blood cells. This would not be permitted today for various health reasons. The girls were not that keen so I volunteered. The lecturer pricked my thumb, put some blood and another liquid on a slide and put the slide under the microscope. He invited me to have a look and tell him what I saw. I related that there were so many red and white cells and black lines moving about.

'Black lines,' he said, with a puzzled look on his face.

He told me there should not be black lines and headed toward my desk. By this time, I was convinced I had some rare, fatal disease and felt a panic attack coming on. He arrived at my desk, looked through the microscope and pulled out the slide.

'You have to wait until the liquid turns into a powder, before you look at it. Did you not hear me say that?'

He could have added 'You numpty.'

Feeling a certain amount of relief, I looked up at him.

'The black lines you see are the liquid moving around as it hasn't dried to a powder yet.' This of course brought laughter from all the girls.

When my year at college was over, I passed my exams with reasonable marks and was back on the job hunt with little success. I now had four Highers and three O-Grades but according to the local Job Centre, that was not enough to impress local employers. I was advised that I could still receive grant funding if I tried for a degree course or an HND so I visited the Mitchell Library and went through the various college and university syllabus material. I ended up applying to Glasgow University for a degree in economic history.

I was accepted for entry to the course some weeks later and an interview with an economics professor was arranged.

I went along with two friends who were also intending to do a degree course at Glasgow. During my interview I tried to get as much information as to the content of the course, what type of job it might lead to and many other questions but the professor just kept saying that since I had the qualifications to get accepted, I would manage out the other side. I had a wife and three children to support and I needed more than his patronising responses to my questions, so I reconsidered my position and decided to look elsewhere. After the interview, I visited the English Department with my friend Margaret. She had been accepted to follow a degree in English and as we walked round looking for her interview room, I noticed that almost every door had a notice, basically telling students to bugger off.

'Please do not put essays under the door',

'Please do not disturb',

'Whatever you need I am sure it can wait until we next meet,' and so on.

I remarked to Margaret that the last thing these professors wanted was to deal with students. She agreed, but nevertheless, that day she took up an offer to study English at Stirling University.

I went back to the Mitchell and found a Higher National Diploma course in Legal Studies, lasting two years, was being offered by Glasgow College of Technology. I noticed the closing date for applications had passed but I went to the college the following day armed with my application form and asked to speak with someone. I was introduced to a lady whom I later came to respect a great deal. During our discussion, she asked why my application was so late. I explained about Glasgow University and my meeting with the professor.

'So, you are rejecting Glasgow University to come here to the Glasgow College of Technology, is that correct?'

'I suppose that's correct if you put it that way,' I said.

'Then you're in. I'll send on the paperwork you'll need and welcome you along to the induction in two weeks.'

I joined the college library that afternoon and visited the law section. I was quite overwhelmed by the number of books they had on the subject and began to get cold feet. I discovered the section with past examination papers and decided to have a look, which was not really a good idea. The lady who had interviewed me, Moira MacMillan, came into the library and spotted me looking through the papers. She came over and asked me if I was starting early. I replied that I may not start at all as what I was reading did not make a lot of sense, to me at least. The exam papers were peppered with Latin phrases which of course I never understood.

'Don't be put off by reading the questions at this stage. You have a year before you'll have to tackle a paper like that.'

I suspect if she had not taken the time to talk with me, I probably would not have turned up for the course. I wrote down one of the questions which I later studied to try and interpret what was required. It was a lengthy piece, but I later worked out it could be reduced to one simple sentence. It was my first lesson in the old adage that when sitting an examination, you should read the question.

The question went along these lines: 'A lorry driver drives out of a pub car park on to a roundabout. He goes the wrong way round and ends up driving the wrong way on a narrow one-way street. A car swerves to avoid the truck and mounts the pavement hitting a worker who is installing a sign outside a shop. The force pushes him through the shop window behind which a window dresser is standing on a ladder. She is knocked over and falls on top of a customer who is about to leave the shop. Across the road on the third floor of a building a window cleaner is washing an office window. The sash cord on the window is broken and he is using his bucket to keep the window open while he cleans the outside. Having witnessed the chaos below he accidently knocks his bucket over and it falls to the ground landing on a passer-by. With nothing to support the window, gravity takes over and the window drops down breaking the window cleaner's wrist.' Then came the instructions: 'Advise the window cleaner.' Once you read this question and understood it thoroughly it was simply saying: 'Discuss the legal principle of Remoteness of Damage.' The principle seeks to limit the claims in a case of negligence to those closely connected with the wrongdoing. Moira was correct, I should not have started reading law questions before I'd learned anything about the subject.

I was registered at Glasgow Technical College but my first week got off to an inauspicious start. The class should have had eighteen hours of lectures but only had two, and one of those took place in the boiler room. Things continued in this vein for the next three weeks but at least the Student Union's Pool Tournament went ahead. I met with a group of students when yet another lecture was cancelled, and told them we shouldn't put up with it and we should lodge a complaint. They were unanimous in agreeing and thought that I should do the complaining to the Head of the Law Department. If he didn't sort it out, we agreed to go above his head, to God, I supposed.

I visited the Department Head's office three or four times but, like our lecturers, he was never available. Finally, I decided an old-fashioned picket was the answer, so I decided I would plant myself in the main office until he turned up. His secretary tried everything she knew to get me to leave but I wasn't wearing it. When I was in the middle of telling her I had been threatened by the police on many a picket line when I worked with the BRS and they couldn't shift me, the Head finally opened his office door and invited me in. I went through the list of lectures where nobody turned up, the number of times rooms had been double-booked and the fact that four weeks into a law course we had not even been told what areas of law we were supposed to begin studying.

He sat there with a disinterested look on his face and when I was finished declared:

'I'm an academic.'

I wasn't sure what he meant by this so I asked him if that meant he couldn't actually do anything practical like sort out a timetable or deal with lecturers' absences. I told him I was travelling by bus leaving at seven-thirty every morning, only to find it was a waste of time and money. I also reminded him that taxpayer's hard-earned money was being used to fund these shambles, and if necessary, I would write to my MP. I think that actually startled him a bit and he asked for my timetable.

'You are timed to have a Legal Procedures lecture at nine tomorrow. Can you advise your fellow students to be there? I will guarantee a lecturer will be available.'

I contacted each student individually and told them to make sure they turned up. He was as good as his word, as were my classmates, so finally we began the study of Scot's law.

In order to take up the offer of a college place I had to sign off from claiming unemployment benefit. My income would now be paid as a student grant, payable in three instalments the first on starting the course. Unfortunately, my grant did not come through on time and I was left with no income. I applied to the Department of Social Security for an 'Urgent Needs Payment,' but was told students could not claim that particular benefit. Which was not strictly true as overseas students could but home students could not. I then suggested the Department arrange a loan that I would pay back but this was also refused. If there's one thing I can say about eventually obtaining an honours degree in law, is that the Social Security did nothing whatsoever to assist me or my family. With no money coming in and no indication when the grant issue would be cleared up, I had two options: leave the course and sign back on, or borrow from friends and seek other sources of help. Among the latter was the Social Work Department who gave my wife a fiver which worked out at a pound a head. My wife recalls she was told if her husband was in prison, they could have offered more assistance but as he was a college student there was not much they could do. I can't remember if I ever paid it back. I also got some help from friends who I did pay back and got a few shifts on the taxis. After five weeks my grant came through, but of course the bank wanted me to wait five days before I could cash it.

I was determined to appeal the decision not to award an Urgent Needs Payment, so I researched the law and lodged an appeal. It was at least three months before the appeal was heard in a Kilmarnock church hall. The lawyer chairman began by reminding me that, regardless of what the Panel decided, the law did not provide for a back-dated payment. I told him I was aware of the rules but nevertheless I was entitled to appeal and make my case on a point of principle. He smiled and indicated that the proceedings should begin. I explained my situation as it was at the time but everything I said was overruled by the representative of the Department of Social Security with his big Yellow Book. The lawyer was clearly trying to assist but his hands and mine were tied by the law. Eventually I asked if I could have a look at his book and the chairman agreed. The Yellow Book in essence was, and probably still is, the Social Security Bible. It sought to outline the rules on all benefits and included decisions of the appeal tribunals and higher courts. I turned to the relevant chapters on Urgent Needs Payments and found an interesting paragraph. It came under the heading of 'Disasters', and whereas elsewhere in the book it was clear that home students were not eligible for such payments, it appeared they could claim if they were affected by a disaster. The Yellow Book defined the word disaster as meaning 'the commonly accepted meaning of the word.' I put it to the

115

chairman that this was a meaningless definition and he agreed to hear arguments. We spent the next couple of hours debating whether having no source of income to feed your wife and family was a disaster. The representative argued the definition meant fire, flood, earthquake and other natural disasters. Every time he used one of these terms, I asked him where in the Yellow Book he had read this definition. He even went on to say that, as I had left the protection of the DHSS by signing off and going to college, it was a self-constituted disaster. After a while the chairman had had enough and declared the proceedings over saying the Panel would issue a decision later. In the end I won my appeal but of course it was a Pyrrhic victory.

To subsidise my grant, I continued working on taxis and ice cream vans and got a job as a furniture delivery driver with MacKay's in Kilwinning, during the summer and at weekends. As it turned out the father of the guy who owned the furniture business was the owner of a few garages and, as a bit of a hobby, ran a wedding-car business. His son asked me if I would be interested in doing some driving for his dad and after the old man gave me a driving test in his 1959 Bentley, he offered me a job driving the wedding cars during the summer. Along with the Bentley and a few other vintage cars, he had a 1970s Rolls Royce, a 1960s Mercedes and a 1930s Hillman that you kicked into life with a starting handle. I had driven all types of cars, vans and trucks over the years but the Hillman took some getting used to. Firstly, you put it into gear, then went outside and turned the starting handle until the engine fired up. Inside and ready to move off, you dipped the clutch in a quick up-and-down movement and the car moved off. When you wanted to change gear, you selected the next highest gear on the steering column gearshift and when the engine noise indicated a gear change was needed, you quickly dipped the clutch up and down. This idea of selecting a gear before you used the clutch flew in the face of everything I had ever driven. But it worked and after a while I got used to it. So much so that later that evening when I went into the manager's Peugeot, I tried to slam it into gear without dipping the clutch, bringing howls of derision.

I got a few shifts driving wedding cars and recall one in particular at Howwood church outside Paisley. I was driving the Hillman and when I heard activity indicating that the ceremony was over, I got out of the car to start it with the starting handle. The doors opened and I heard a voice say,

'Oh my God, the car's broken down.'

I assured the guest who had called out that there was nothing wrong with the car and that was how you started it normally. Suddenly I was surrounded by a number of male guests who wanted to know more about how it worked. I was in the process of explaining the system of first selecting a gear and then turning the starting handle until the engine sparked into life. As I continued a quite effeminate voice almost screamed for the bridegroom and the best man to get into line so he could take their photographs. When I asked him if he wanted a photograph of the bride and groom seated in the car, he practically tore my hair out. In the end, he agreed it would make a nice shot. I wonder how long the married couple stayed together after he revealed more interest in the vintage car than getting his wedding photographs taken.

On another occasion, after a shift in the furniture van, Angus said he would drive me to the garage at Barrhead to pick up the Rolls Royce and take it to his dad's house in Uplawmoor. As I was driving through Barrhead, I discovered I was out of cigarettes. I also remembered that Angus had still to pay me for the week and I had very little money. I finally scraped up enough for ten cigarettes and went into the shop.

'Ten Embassy Regal please,' I said to the shopkeeper who gave me such a look of disdain. He was probably expecting me to be spending a few quid when he saw me coming out of the Roller. The old man McKay had recently had it re-sprayed a burgundy colour with new matching upholstery. When you removed the white wedding bands from the bonnet and the flowers from the back window there was nothing to suggest it was a wedding car or that I was just a chauffeur. The old man later decided to retire and sold his vintage cars. The garage was bought over and turned into the Hurlet Hotel where it remained for a long time before closing down.

The furniture business continued under his son and one Saturday morning I drove to Perth to carry out a removal. Angus suggested I use the smaller van as he had estimated the removal himself and there was not a lot of furniture. He was right about the furniture in the flat but he hadn't looked in the garage where the shrewd customer had stored a load of white goods including a freezer, fridge, washing machine, tumble drier, as well as a three-piece suite, a bed and a load of boxes. I actually had to put some odds and ends in the cab as I couldn't get the back door shut. Angus would not admit he had been conned with the estimate and suggested I hadn't packed it properly. I had packed more trucks and vans than he'd had hot dinners. Business was beginning to slow down, especially the delivery contract with Cantors furniture shop in Irvine. There was a rumour that it was about to close and indeed it did. I wasn't surprised by this as I thought most of what they sold was rather poorly-made stuff. When you pack a three-piece suite in a van you put the armchairs on their side one on top of the other, stand the sofa on its side against them, cover all with a blanket and tie the whole lot to the side of the truck using a canvas strap. On more than one occasion when I pulled the strap tight, I heard a crack and discovered the wooden support across the front of the couch had broken. However, the loss of my job with the furniture removals was not that big a deal. I could still turn a shilling driving taxis and ice-cream vans and I was now quite friendly with a local Labour councillor who worked as a plasterer. He often gave me a shift labouring for him, usually roughcasting private houses. He seemed averse to working after lunchtime so he kept going nonstop during the morning. He still tells people the story of when he was up the ladders plastering away and I shouted to him:

'What's the difference between a Labour boss and a Tory boss?' He could not come up with an answer.

'You get a fucking tea break with a Tory!' I shouted back.

I think in the long term we spent more time arguing over politics than plastering. During the Miner's Strike of 1984 we were involved in collecting food and other items for an appeal run by a local newspaper, *The Irvine Herald*. Most people were very supportive, but we were subject to the odd shouting match in the street from the odd Thatcherite. I think it was around that time I swore I would outlive that fucking woman and I'm glad I achieved that ambition. When she died there was singing and dancing at George Square and the BBC in its usual impartial fashion would not play *The Wicked Witch is Dead*.

It was whilst working as a labourer that I began to suffer pain in both knees and after numerous tests was diagnosed as having arthritis. This spread to my lower back and although I felt able to continue working, I was advised by my doctor that I would not be able to pass the medical for the renewal of my Heavy Goods Licence, which was due when I turned forty. So, looking for full-time work back on the lorries was out of the question.

Chapter Nine

Mature Student 1980s

It was June 1986 when I completed my HND successfully, but I was nowhere near obtaining a good, permanent job. One was advertised in the Job Centre that I thought would suit me very well. Renfrewshire Council advertised for someone with an HGV Licence and a legal qualification. I figured there could not be too many people who met this criterion and I applied but didn't even get an interview.

The Council was setting up a mobile welfare benefits information service, along the lines of a mobile library. I had the driving experience, of course, and I also had some experience of the social security system having represented a number of people at various appeals. I had also represented workers at what is now termed an Employment Tribunal. The Labour Government under Blair changed the title from 'Industrial Tribunal', lest anyone got the daft idea that we had an industry left in Britain. They would also change the references to social welfare by introducing the Department of Work and Pensions to replace the Department of Social Security.

I had one offer of a job as a Precognition Agent. This involved speaking with witnesses about what they claim to have seen or heard in a criminal or civil case. It requires the ability to record accurately what you are told regardless of how poor the person's grammar may be or the fact that they may use local expressions for everyday items, known by another name elsewhere. After thinking it over I honestly did not relish going into a housing estate on a dark evening

120

to interview 'Mad Dog' McGurn about his alleged assault of three police officers, so I declined.

I found myself being asked to help with advice on faulty goods, wills and other general legal stuff, which kept me busy reading and writing for a while. I worked with Adult Basic Education which was rewarding but unpaid. I remember my first student simply wanted to learn to write, chiefly because she wanted to communicate with her brother who was in Australia. A couple of days after she had her first lesson, I saw her in the street along with a man I presumed was her husband. I was on the verge of saying hello when she pulled him into a shop and indicated I shouldn't say anything. At her next lesson she explained that she hadn't told her husband she was going to ABE and if she'd said hello, he would have asked too many questions. Who was I? How did she know me? and so on. I was quite taken aback that she seemed to be ashamed of being unable to read and write.

A few months later she wrote to her brother. We both laughed at his reply because the first thing he asked her was who wrote the letter for her? I remember also having a young man who simply wanted to be able to write numbers as words. He was running his own disco business and was getting a lot of work. He had been advised to keep accounts for tax purposes and to pay any expenses by writing a cheque but he could not express a sum like £17.54p in words. I asked him if he was ever asked in writing to play a particular song and he said he did.

'So, what do you do if you can't read it?' I asked.

His reply was that he just made out the person was a bad writer. In essence he covered up his own embarrassment by embarrassing someone else. I came across multiple examples of people who blamed themselves for their inability to read and write and I could not understand how they got through the world. My father had very poor reading and writing skills but he had left school when he was twelve. I remember when he wrote out a line for the bookies, he copied what he saw in the newspaper rather than read the horse's name and write it freehand. I attended an adult education conference in Belmont Academy, Ayr, and learned about dyslexia and its arithmetical equivalent, dyscalculus. It was an informative experience after which I became very conscious that the ability to read and write is a gift that we should cherish.

Out of the blue I was offered an interview for a job with a firm of solicitors in St. Vincent Street in Glasgow. I was called into an office where three people were sat behind a large desk one of whom introduced me to the senior partner when he arrived late. This individual, who was quite pompous, went on to advise that the firm had contacted Glasgow Technical College looking for a student who was familiar with the process of 'Calling up Mortgages', a fancy term for evicting people if they default on their mortgage and cannot pay.

'I'm not interested in a debt collecting job,' I said.

His reaction surprised me.

'Do you not believe people should pay what they owe?' he asked.

'People get into debt because they really can't afford to buy a house but they need one,' I said. 'People like you arrange a mortgage based on two salaries, then she gets pregnant and he loses his job. Game over. When that happens, you bow out and people like me call up their mortgage by following certain legal processes. It's debt collecting. When you strip away the fancy language, calling up mortgages is debt collecting, pure and simple.'

Following a short debate, he asked me why I was so against debt collecting.

'Have you ever woken up on a Monday morning without the price of a loaf?' I asked.

In his pompous manner, he replied he had not.

'Well I have,' I said, and rose to leave. 'If you ever have a job for someone who wants to assist those with debt problems let me know,' I said in parting.

He never did. I went to the college after the interview and spoke with staff in the Law Department. I thanked them for giving me such a splendid reference but told them never to recommend me for a debt collecting job again.

After applying for a number of lecturing posts I got a call from the Head of Business Studies at Kilmarnock College. A course at the Bank Street Annex in Irvine was oversubscribed and another class was put together. This meant he needed someone to teach an employment law module at very short notice. I went to see him that Friday afternoon and it was agreed I would take the second class from the following Thursday. I produced a set of lecture notes and arrived in good time for my first ever paid lecture.

There was about sixteen in the class over a broad age range. Their main subject of study was Travel and Tourism, which was aimed at people wanting to work in the holiday business. The course included a trip to Spain, which I suspect was why it was oversubscribed. I was made aware that the decision to include an employment law module was not met with enthusiasm among the students and they would probably ask why they had to learn this subject. In fact, that was among the first questions asked when I was outlining what we would be covering every Thursday for the next three months. I advised them that in my view all knowledge had value and maybe someday, when their boss was giving them a hard time in the travel agency, they would be thankful they knew their rights at work.

However, they were clearly unimpressed so I sent them for a break. On their return it was clear their lack of enthusiasm had not waned. When they were seated and staring forward with that 'So, teach me' look, I turned my back on them, rolled down the chalk board and wrote 'FUCK OFF' across it in large letters. I turned, threw the chalk on my desk and looked at their silent faces.

'Now!' I said, 'If your boss ever tells you to fuck off, the question is: what do these words mean in law? Are you dismissed? In a case entitled Futty versus Brekkes in 1974, that was indeed the question the Law Lords sought to answer. Futty gutted fish on Hull docks. One day he complained that the fish were too small for filleting and his boss told him if he didn't like it, he could "fuck off". Futty did exactly that, and later claimed at a tribunal that he was entitled to dismiss himself and claim constructive dismissal.'

When most of the class began to ask questions on what I had just said, I knew I had them a bit more enthusiastic about the law. When you look at that actual decision it shows how class-ridden the legal system was in the 1970s and it is probably much the same today. For example, one judge remarked that if someone like a bank manager had told an employee to 'fuck off' that would constitute dismissal but as these words were used in a fish market among common workers who used that language regularly, it did not. What pretentious tripe!

I really enjoyed my three months at Bank Street and was sad when it ended but they vowed not to oversubscribe the next course. I did get a short period of employment teaching business law at Stow College in Glasgow but it was only filling-in for illness. Neither of these short-term teaching jobs led to full-time work so aged 48 I went back into full-time education.

Glasgow Technical College was now known as Glasgow Caledonian University and was offering a BA degree in Law and Public Administration. I still had two years of a student grant available so I applied and was accepted. I entered at the third-year level and gained my degree with distinction at the end of that year. I was then invited to proceed to the Honour's year and graduated with a 2:1 Honours Degree when I was fifty. During those two years I made many friends among the students, most of whom were less than half my age.

The only work experience the younger students had gained in their life so far was bar and restaurant work, shop assistant and the like, mostly during holidays. They would 'sleep in' for a lecture at eleven and I found it hilarious. I used to ask them how they would manage in the world of work.

'If you get a full-time job your boss won't tolerate you arriving late every morning like you do in here.' I used to tell them, but they just laughed it off.

As it turned out many of them did get jobs and did rather well in fact. The lecturers were a mixed bunch but for the most part extremely helpful and interesting. Lectures on Friday afternoons were usually the most interesting owing to the odd liquid lunch being consumed, by the lecturers not the students.

One Friday a notice was posted stating that a certain lecturer had our examination dates and subject information obtainable from his office. I went along with fellow student, Althea, to get the paperwork for our class, but his office was locked. We were standing outside in the corridor when I told her he was coming along and he was drunk.

'How do you know he's drunk?' She asked.

I pointed out that the double doors along the corridor each had a small window and you could see him in one window then the other then the other, all the way along the corridor. Finally, he burst through the last set of doors and spotted us leaning against the wall.

'Ah, Mr Keeman and Miss McGhee, are you looking for me?'

We explained about the paperwork and he invited us into his office. There was a large bundle of computer printouts on top of a cabinet which he lifted and simultaneously dropped all over the floor. I told Althea to pick them up and I would deal with him. I bundled him into his chair and he reached forward, opened a desk drawer, pulled out a bottle of Scotch and offered us a drink.

'You're pissed,' I told him.

'And you are one of my more observant students,' he fired back sarcastically.

I phoned him a taxi and we bundled him down the back stairs and into the cab. The following week he never mentioned the episode and I don't think he ever did, even when we had the odd pint together.

European Law was a large part of our studies and a fellow student explained she was having difficulty finding a particular case. The facts were that a London defendant tried to use the European law on free movement of goods to defend himself on a criminal charge of importing pornographic material from Holland into England. I remembered the case as I thought it was a novel defence at the time and I knew it was in the English Appeal Court citations in the library. To my surprise, if not horror, she did not know where to find the law section of the library, saying she relied on the recommended text book and lecture notes. In the third year of a law degree and she never used the library, astonishing! We went to the library and I was going through the index of a casebook of English law whilst she looked over my shoulder.

'That Regina is involved in a lot of cases,' she said. I turned round expecting to see her laughing at her own joke, but it wasn't a joke.

'Maybe you should visit the library more often,' I suggested.

Nevertheless, she left at the end of the year with an ordinary degree and we later heard she was working as a para-legal with a law firm.

Just before we broke for the Christmas holidays in 1994, I had a meeting with my supervisor to discuss possible topics for my dissertation. He was unsure whether to accept my topic as it was criminal law rather than civil law, which took up most of the course. He said he felt I may have insufficient knowledge of criminal law to complete a fifteen-thousand-word thesis and he asked what my idea was.

'Juries,' I said. I went on to explain I had served as the Foreman on two juries at Kilmarnock Sheriff Court and was interested in how juries arrived at their decisions, what they really understood by the 'Not Proven' verdict, and terms like self-defence, impeachment and other legal jargon, tossed around by lawyers without explanation.

'There hasn't been a lot of academic writing on juries in the context you are considering. Have you thought about your approach to obtaining the type of information you will need?' he asked.

I swear he almost fell off his chair when I suggested I would advertise for people who had served on a jury to complete a questionnaire.

'That is illegal. You cannot discuss with any jury member how they arrived at their decision or anything else that was discussed in the jury room.'

'I know,' I said, 'It's contempt of court but I figured if I'm arrested the university will provide funds for a legal defence. Academic freedom - that's my legal defence.'

I could see he didn't know whether to laugh or greet.

'John,' he said. 'This isn't Oxford or Cambridge, and as for a legal defence fund you can forget it. Now I suggest you choose an alternative topic so we can move on. I'm sure you have one lurking in that devious mind of yours.'

I opened my bag and took out a file. 'Capital Punishment,' I said. 'I've looked through a list of titles of previous dissertations and it does not appear to have been the subject of a thesis recently. The Not Proven verdict seems to be the hot topic followed by the civil case of *Donohue v Stevenson*.'

He nodded and expressed the view that I should remember to stick to the legal aspects as he did not want to read some sort of sociology essay about cruel and unusual punishment. I already had a title written down and chose to run it past him.

The thing about dissertation titles is to make them long winded and a bit pretentious. So, I read it out: 'A Critical Examination of the Proposal that the Restoration of the Death Penalty into UK Law would provide a Deterrent to Murder.'

'Sounds interesting,' he said. 'I suggest you lay out some sort of structure, chapter plan if you like, and I'll see you some time after the Easter Holidays when we can go through it.'

It was my intention to do my research during the holidays, and as the UK no longer used the death penalty the Home Office could provide little useful information. However, the death penalty still remained on the statute books for what Amnesty International described as 'exceptional crimes'. In Britain those amounted to certain treasonable acts and offences under the provisions of the Armed Services Act 1971 and the Army Act 1955. In search of information I turned to the United States. I wrote to Amnesty International in New York; the Death Penalty Information Centre in Washington; the American Civil Liberties Union in New York; and the FBI, from whom I received a constant stream of statistical information. Among the many statistics was one that claimed that in most of the states that used the death penalty, the murder rate rose in the weeks following an execution. The writers argued in their research paper that executions sent a message to people that human life was pretty worthless.

When I returned to university after the holidays my dissertation was almost complete. My fear that I could not write fifteen-thousand-words on a single subject proved unfounded. In fact, great chunks had to be removed, but it achieved a good mark and better still those who read it, including my supervisor, said it was a good read. With that task completed I could afford to relax and devote some extra time to my final exams.

Janet and my two oldest sons, John and James, came to

the Graduation Ceremony in the Glasgow Concert Hall and were suitably bored. I was thinking of giving it a miss myself but I received a telephone call saying I had been selected as top student of that year by my fellow classmates and lecturers. This was indeed a real surprise as was the fifty quid that went with the selection.

With the fifty quid spent and the celebrations over it was back to signing-on and looking for work. During a visit to my local Job Centre I was discussing a particular vacancy with a careers advisor who asked me what qualifications I had. Years before when I was asked this question the answer was none and that was seen as a major stumbling block to getting work. Now when I rhymed off my certificates it was suggested that I was over-qualified for the job. The advisor suggested that the employer would probably think, with the qualifications I had, I would be constantly looking for a better job and therefore be reluctant to employ me. When he suggested I leave out my Honours Degree and go with the HND and Highers only, I told him to do the same as Mr Futty was told to do when he complained about the size of fish in the market in Hull.

Shortly after I graduated, I got a call from one of my previous fellow students who asked if we could meet. We met in the refectory at Glasgow Caledonian University. Over tea and coffee, he told me he had a place at Strathclyde University to study for a Master's degree in European Law, but there was an issue with a course advisor. The advisor was recommending he study for a diploma rather than the degree programme as he felt the latter would present him with difficulties. I asked my friend what career path he was looking to follow and he said he wanted to become a law lecturer, specialising in European Law. When I established that what he'd been told was simply that individual's personal opinion, I advised him to insist he wanted to study for the Master's. If he failed that would be that, but he was not going to drop his expectations on the opinion of one person. I told him I would help him where I could and we'd see how things went.

The day before his European Law exam some months later I had him down to my house in Irvine. From ten in the morning until ten at night we went through past exam papers, text books, and notes, pausing only briefly for lunch and supper. Janet, who was taking care of the food and drink, told me more than once to 'give the poor boy a break,' but we carried on until I drove him to the station to catch the last train home. In the end he qualified with his Master's Degree and did get a lecturing position at a Glasgow College. As a reward for my efforts he paid for tickets for us both to see Billy Connolly at the King's Theatre. Being back in his home territory, the Big Yin was in great form and had the audience in stitches for hours.

Graduation 1980s

Chapter Ten

A Whole New Career 1990s

At the beginning of 1996 I found myself back at university, this time in Paisley. I had found a grant-funded computer course designed for degree students with no formal computer knowledge. Any degree, apart from a degree in computing of course, qualified you for entry, so I applied and was accepted. Early on in the course I attended a lecture by a Japanese computer expert in a room with about two or three hundred students. He may as well have delivered the lecture in Japanese for all I understood. Apparently, he was talking about the philosophy of computing according to a fellow student.

I had just spent two years studying, among other things, Jurisprudence –the philosophy of law. If you ever feel like having your whole brain twisted and turned until you don't know whether it's in your arse or your head, try reading some Scandinavian 'legal realism' by Herebert Olivecrona or Axel Hagerstrom. You could also try Saint Thomas Aquinas' Natural Law theory or even Hohfeld's analysis with its jural opposites and jural correlatives and distinctions between a right, a claim, a privilege and an immunity. 'Are you still with me?' No! I'd had enough studying and I needed a job in the real world, whether it existed or not.

During my last year at Caledonian, a fellow student, who had left the year before to take up a position with the Citizens' Advice Bureau, contacted me to say she had left and was now working as an advisor with a new organisation known as the BBC Radio Helpline. She said she thought I

131

would love the work and suggested I call for an application form. At that time, I was busy studying and I told her I was not intending to look for work until I had finished my final year. A few months after my graduation, I was finding the computer course tedious and phoned my former student colleague. I asked if they were still recruiting at Helpline and she suggested I send them a CV. I sent it off but never received a response so I sent another.

This time I received a letter inviting me for an interview and containing a legal question relating to domestic violence, with a request for a written answer to be sent before I attended. I complied, of course, and was invited to Breckinridge House on Sauchiehall Street, next door to the MacLellan Galleries. The interview was in the evening and lasted around four hours. There was a group of people who were interviewees and another group who were Helpline staff. Everyone had a one-to-one and we were put into discussion groups and given a variety of topics to discuss. The concluding part involved making an audio tape of your own choice. You could read a poem or something from a book, or deliver a rant on some personal detestation. I chose to read the question on domestic violence and my answer. By the time I got near to the end of the tape I was convinced I would not get a job, so I finished by saying: 'John Keeman, BBC Radio Helpline, Sauchiehall Street, Glasgow, and it's a goodnight from me and it's goodnight from him.' In the end my judgment was wrong and I got a letter asking me to attend at the Theatre Royal on Hope Street to begin my training in late February, 1996.

During that week we covered a number of topics including telephone skills, writing skills and research skills. This was before the internet so we also received library training and a brief introduction to the BBC Radio Helpline's history. With all of the trainees being university graduates the training was not too taxing and the surroundings of the old theatre provided an atmospheric environment.

Since the 1930s the BBC had offered support and information to their audience but this was generally short term. The new Helpline however, was a permanent twenty-four-hour service. It was funded, at a cost of around five million pounds a year. In its first few years it had over a hundred contracted staff full and part-time; it also had a bank of sessional workers and specialists from statutory and voluntary agencies, like the Employment Services, Citizens' Advice, Bereavement and other charities. All staff, including those from other bodies, received BBC training with emphasis on caller anonymity, impartiality, and confidentiality. Staff were bound by the BBC Producers Guidelines and trained to provide objective information to those who called Helpline. Most internal and external staff had specific specialisms which was useful when briefing sheets were being produced to enable them to answer calls.

The training also covered the two main objectives of Helpline, firstly to provide a source of accurate information to listeners responding to programmes on BBC Radio, and secondly, to provide feedback reports to programme makers about the interests and concerns of their audiences. Statistical information was sought from callers as to their gender, age and area of the country they were calling from, but names and other personal information was never sought for these reports. One producer was quoted as saying: 'The Helpline reports have provided a valuable insight as to who the listener actually is and what they think about our programmes.'

The main part of the job was to provide the audience with further information on a particular topic discussed on air. Health issues, including mental health, accounted for about four-in-ten of calls. The remainder was made up of consumer issues, finance, debt and benefit problems, relationships, education and employment, legal matters, environment and leisure. In fact, anything heard on a radio programme on any of the five major networks could result in an enquiry from a listener, if the programme gave out the network's number. Information to answer calls was sourced from Briefing Sheets compiled by the same staff who took listeners' calls. The information for these sheets was sourced from charities, the programme synopsis, programme guests, CAB files and specialists on the particular topic. Briefing Sheets also included contact details for charities and other institutions where further, more detailed information, could be accessed by callers.

Following the week at the Theatre Royal I was invited to another training course this time in the Ingram Hotel in Glasgow. Here, one Sunday afternoon, we met BBC programme makers who spoke about their role within the BBC and went through the BBC Producers Guidelines. Great emphasis was placed on taking an objective, impartial and non-judgmental approach when speaking with their audiences. It was a very interesting insight into the BBC and the food was most pleasant. The next step in my training was a two-day conference at the Caledonian Hotel in Ayr and it began on one of the blackest days in Scotland's history.

On March 13th, 1996, Thomas Hamilton, described on BBC News as 'a middle-aged loner, fixated on youngsters, guns and his own grievances', killed sixteen children and their teacher and then committed suicide, in the Scottish town of Dunblane. It was devastating news and we watched BBC Scotland as it reported every minute. Those full-time staff, who were overseeing the conference, cancelled the day's agenda and began setting up a helpline, staffed by bereavement counsellors with referral numbers for organisations who could provide counselling and a listening ear. I was very moved by their genuine concerns and impressed by how quickly telephone lines were set up, contact made with appropriate organisations and staff called in to answer the calls. I knew then this was an organisation I wanted to work with.

By the 25th of March I had completed my induction training and three weeks later I was still waiting for news about actual work. Eventually it came and I was called in for my first shift from three-fifteen until ten-fifteen. I was a little bit fortunate with my calls that evening. Radio 4 was trailing their number during a campaign on welfare benefits and at that time I was involved with North Ayrshire's Welfare Rights group in a social security appeal. This involved a number of disabled claimants, and I had quite an extensive knowledge of the benefits system at the time. Consequently, I did not find the calls too difficult to handle. I got a very good report from the supervisor with the negative being that I kept forgetting to ask callers for their age group, area and gender.

My work, being in the evenings and weekends, left me free to continue with some other interests and, in April, I was advising a former student friend on how to recover her deposit from a landlord in Airdrie. From my personal experience the most troubling aspect of student life was trying to recover their deposits when they were moving on. Landlords always claimed they had left the place in a mess and consequently were justified in keeping the deposit. However, when we sent this particular landlord a summons for a Small Claims Action to be raised in Airdrie Sheriff Court, the deposit was returned in full. But I was not as successful in a Social Security Appeal at the Court of Session in Edinburgh.

In that case I was involved on behalf of my son, John, and other disabled claimants. The assembled audience in court included Welfare Rights Officers, representatives from charitable groups, and lawyers from various legal centres. We were present as we had an interest in Carrington Case, that involved payment of a benefit known as a Severe Disability Premium. Disabled persons could claim this benefit under certain circumstances but the Government kept moving the

135

goalposts. Consequently, a series of court cases arose with charitable organisations, welfare rights groups and others challenging decisions made by the Department of Health and Social Security. On the day of the hearing it became quite clear to all of us that we were fighting a losing battle and when it ended, we retired to the Scotsman's Lounge in Cockburn Street. Two of the Advocates for our side accompanied us and opined that the judgment would likely go against us.

'However,' one of them said, 'We have embarrassed the Government in court today.'

I could not listen to this tripe anymore and told him that firstly Governments do not get embarrassed and secondly claimants could not spend embarrassment at Tesco. They both left soon after and the rest of us stayed and discussed further tactics in this ongoing battle that eventually took six years to resolve.

By the end of April, I was getting regular shifts at the Helpline and worked most weekends which meant giving up my taxi and ice cream van jobs but even on a three or four shift week I could earn enough to pay the bills, have a beer and a bet on the horses.

Around my third month I had a meeting with the Radio 4 Liaison Officer. Each network had one of these grandly-titled officers whose basic job was to encourage programme makers to use the service, ensure producers got their feedback reports, and handle any complaints about the service, or indeed about the BBC. I met with a young woman called Jane, who suggested there were some programmes on Radio 4 that discussed issues that were within my areas of interest and experience. She suggested I was given access to the Radio 4 schedules database. With these sources of information on forthcoming programmes I could select those I thought could benefit from using the Helpline, phone the producers and discuss using the service. I told her I was a little bit hesitant to speak with programme makers, being very new to the service.

'The BBC is a doing organisation John,' she said. 'If you think you have something to contribute just do it. If it works well, then good, if it doesn't move on.'

I've struggled to convince a few producers on Radio 4 to use the service because they feel they are not making social action programmes. *Law in Action* simply said we are not a consumer programme. 'We are not *You and Yours*,' they said.

Pretentious twats.

In the end she said she could arrange some time off the telephones for me to do this work and suggested when the Helpline was recruiting for full-time staff the experience would stand me in good stead. So, I agreed to give it a try. In fact, I enjoyed contacting producers with ideas for a Helpline programme and had some success which I think was due to my knowledge of the network. When I first listened to Radio 4 it was called 'The Home Service.' There was no Radio One or 5-Live and Radio Two was known as 'The Light Programme,' with Radio Three going by the bland title of 'The Third Programme.' As a young kid I listened to the wireless every night and during the day. I listened to *Workers Playtime* at lunchtime on the Light Programme and drama on the Home Service at night and comedy shows like *Amos and Andy*. Even to this day I still prefer listening to a radio drama rather than watching television, and thanks to the modern technology my wife loves to hate, I can listen to plays from all over the world on my mobile phone.

The year progressed quickly and I was on an ever-climbing learning curve. I was tasked with writing briefing sheets where the topic included some legal issue which was a wide-ranging area: consumerism, debt, employment, personal injury, benefits, domestic violence, divorce and wills. I recall that the *Jimmy Young Show* on Radio Two did a piece on writing your own will which attracted thousands of calls. At the end of the year I finally accepted that my time at university had not been wasted. At the age of fifty-two I was following a completely different line of work that I found very satisfying and rewarding. I looked forward to the New Year and new challenges, as the old year faded.

Early in the New Year Lord MacLean delivered his decision in the Carrington Case. It was as we suspected and we were back to exploring other avenues of appeal. It was clear that the Department of Health and Social Security were determined to pay as few claimants as possible. After one successful appeal by a claimant, the Minister for Social Security appeared in Parliament about ten hours after the court's judgment and enacted a Statutory Instrument that neutered the decision. The suspicion, among many of us, was that he had advised DHSS offices across the country before he had advised Parliament after midnight that evening. We arrived at this conclusion because these offices were aware of the decision at opening time on the day following the decision which was given by the judges at four-thirty the previous day, when most DHSS Offices were closed. When we challenged the Minister on this, his reply was that the offices had fax machines.

Of course, we had become used to the Department acting against their own guidelines but got nowhere when we questioned this and the Government seemed to get special treatment from the Social Security Commissioners in Edinburgh, who did not seem to us to be the pinnacle of independent thinking. On one occasion the Commissioners wrote to me saying they wanted to suspend a decision on an appeal until a certain case was concluded in the House of Lords. Their letter stated that if I was unhappy with this I could object. I wrote outlining a number of objections and reminding them that their own guidelines required them to act speedily in making their decisions and requested that they make a decision timeously. In response to my letter I got a Mister Humphrey's response stating that they had suspended any decision on my objections. A blatant example of bias if ever I saw one.

At one point I considered bringing a Small Claims Action against the Minister but my son's lawyer did not think it would work. However, he was a bit more enthusiastic when I suggested petitioning the European Court of Human Rights on the grounds that the British Government had acted illegally in the administration of this particular benefit. He said he was not all that familiar with the European Court but offered me assistance if I wanted to research the option. Over the next couple of months, I devoted as much time as I could to this project.

Within a year of starting as a sessional worker with the Helpline I was successful in obtaining a full-time position. This involved working from 'nine 'til five - what a way to make a living.' Television programmes were now encouraged to use the service and we supported broadcasts on BBC One, including *Panorama, Watchdog, Crimewatch*, breakfast television, *Horizon* on BBC Two and other major broadcasts. Support for television programmes was one of the topics discussed at a meeting that I was asked to attend in a well-known hotel in Inverary.

On the first day we finished our meeting around four o'clock when some of us went into the bar. One of the hotel chefs handed round menus for the evening meal and after a look I handed mine over the bar. The chef asked me if I saw anything I liked and I told him I had not read any French since I left school and besides, I never ate anything I couldn't pronounce. He laughed and asked me what kind of food I liked and I told him I was very partial to steak pie with sausages, jacket potatoes and butter with fresh green peas. Later that evening about twenty of us were sat around a large dining table as staff served up the evening meals. They were a mixture of salmon or chicken covered in some sort of fancy sauce and most of them looked banal and not very appetizing.

Suddenly the chef appeared at my shoulder carrying a silver salver. When he removed the top, he revealed a steak pie and pastry in a stone ashet, jacket potatoes with butter and sprinkles of parsley and fresh green peas.

'It's a poor chef who can't rustle up a bit of steak pie,' he said.

My thought was if this tastes as good as it looks it will be delicious. And it did. The pie also gave rise to a number of comments, mostly about it not being on the menu.

'If you don't ask you don't get,' I told them, feeling very smug indeed.

Over the next few months, I researched literally hundreds of topics mostly with a legal aspect. I recall Credit Reference Agreements for a debt campaign, electronic tagging, European employment laws and so on. In March I attended a law course in London run by the 'Legal Action Group.'

It was a series of lectures over two days delivered by two law professors from Bristol University. The major topic was the Police and Criminal Evidence Act, or 'PACE' as it was colloquially known on television dramas like *The Bill*. The course was designed for English solicitors to bring them up to date with suspects' rights when being questioned over arrestable and non-arrestable offences. There were about a dozen lawyers present and when some of us went outside for a smoke, a couple of them asked me about the Scottish 'Not Proven' verdict.

Firstly, I said it meant 'We know you done it but we can't prove it so you're free to go.'

But collectively they spotted a flaw in this explanation so I asked them what they thought it meant. For the first, and perhaps the only time in my life, I witnessed four or five lawyers actually agreeing to the same thing. What made it more interesting was they were all wrong. They thought it meant an accused found 'Not Proven', could be tried again if new evidence came to light. When I pointed out the verdict had the same effect on the accused as a 'Not Guilty,' they said they didn't see the sense in having it. I told them there were many people in Scotland who held the same opinion.

London, as ever, was a great place to visit but I could never live there for any more than four or five days at a time. Outside of work I was dealing with an interesting claim for damages on behalf of a friend. He was walking in Montgomerie Street in Irvine when a weather vane fell from a building. It hit the wall a few times before landing on his head and then his right knee damaging both. The injuries were not severe but the person he was with had the presence of mind to photograph the weather vane and injuries and report it to the local authority. In fact, they took the weather vane home and called the council to come and collect it and made an appointment to see a doctor. My friend asked me if I would write a letter for him so I contacted the Council's insurers. They responded by denying liability so I sent them a copy of a Small Claims Court Summons, saying I would have it warranted and served on them if they did not respond with a reasonable offer within fourteen days. Thankfully common sense prevailed and they paid up. It was a local authority building and they had put the weather vane up on the roof. The fact that the insurers sought to deny liability was, in my view, absurd and time wasting, but what else can you expect from insurers?

Having some knowledge of consumer and personal injury law was instrumental in my being tasked with writing briefing sheets for various radio and television broadcasts, including *Watchdog*, a programme that attracted thousands of calls. It was essential that viewers were given accurate information and a procedure was put into place to ensure this. We reached an agreement with the Trading Standards Institute which involved a consumer law expert. When *Watchdog* sent me their programme information, I called the expert and discussed each area of law involved and relevant referral agencies. I then drafted a briefing sheet which I sent to the expert and he came back with any amendments or corrections before it was put into our computer system. Coupled with this I put together a training course designed to give staff a basic background in consumer law. The process worked very well and was in use until I retired.

The expert was a very nice guy, for a lawyer, and we got on well but we had never met face to face, all contact being by telephone or email. Many months after we discussed our first *Watchdog* broadcast, I was at a consumer conference in Queen Elizabeth II Conference Centre near Westminster Abbey. As I was being signed in, an instantly recognizable voice piped up:

'You're buying a load of trouble if you let him in. He's one of those Scotsmen who stole our goalposts.'

It was my legal expert. He was, of course, referring to a particular England v Scotland international football match that Scotland won, leading their fans to take parts of the pitch and goalposts home with them. I had nothing to do with this of course but it was a standing joke between us that I should arrange for their return.

Later that afternoon we went to a pub to meet some of his friends and colleagues who included a number of MPs and the Director General of the Office of Fair Trading. The latter told me a story about a man who bought a carpet and laid it himself. He set one end against the wall, rolled the carpet out a couple of feet and tacked it down. He repeated this process about half a dozen times until, when he got to the other side, he discovered it was too short for the room. He ripped it up, tacks and all and took it back to the seller demanding a refund. The seller refused and the buyer raised a small claims action but before the court case started a deal was made. However, the seller did not advise his lawyer that the case was settled and the lawyer arrived in court to find this out from the clerk. This farce so annoyed the judge that he made an order saying the Director General should investigate the carpet seller's business practices. So, there he was: the grandly entitled Director General of the Office of Fair Trading, investigating the case of the two-feet-short carpet.

It was a memorable day but further evidence that I could never stay in London; everyone in that pub was wound up planning and plotting all sorts of business ideas, investment possibilities, property developments, most of which I'm sure never saw the light of day. But I had enough material for the work's magazine, a weekly production that took the piss out of as many staff as possible. If you got a mention in *The Stun* you were allocated a new name. I was Professor Keenman, Lyn Harvie, the assistant director, became Lyn Hair-Do, my red-haired friend was Ginger Twat, we had a Murdo MacBurger, Captain Chaos, Mister Tasty and others. The idea of *The Stun* was to boost staff moral and give them something to laugh about in an organisation that took a very high number of sad and disturbing calls from very distressed people. People who had loved ones murdered, people who had been given very bad news about their health, people who had suffered bereavement, people who were being bullied and suffering in other ways. I penned this piece for *The Stun* as a sort of satire on Watchdog.

Grinding Voice: 'Hello Good Evening and Welcome to Growler. Live from Television Centre. This is the number everyone's trying to ring but only middle-class twits from Weybridge can get through. Tonight, we report on how Mister Average Consumer from Weybridge couldn't get satisfaction until Growler stepped in. Mister A was driving his £25,634 Mercedes when his £200 Rayban sunglasses fell over his eyes whilst he was on a £19,000 holiday in Barbados. The impact of the crash damaged his £245 mobile phone and his £500 pocket computer. To make matters worse when he returned home his £2,600 landscape gardening job was

143

flooded by Thames Water and there was a letter from an airline telling him he couldn't get his favourite window seat on his next £1500 flight to Florida and to crown it all his PVC trousers had gone baggy at the knees. But when Growler stepped in everything in the garden turned rosy.' 'Growler the programme that looks after your average consumer. So! get out there! complain! Make a fuss! 'Average Consumer 'Oh F--- O— Annie.'

These were genuine items complained about on the programme but to me they were not complaints by the 'average' consumer. In my view if you can afford to pay two-hundred pounds for a pair of sunglasses you could afford to pay a lawyer to sort out your consumer problems, rather than calling a social action helpline. That is a partial and judgmental view I agree.

Amongst other things I assisted colleagues and friends with their own consumer problems. One in particular involved my wife's friend Martha, who had bought a new marble fireplace. The sellers delivered and installed it and went on their way. A few weeks later Martha was sitting with her husband in front of the fire watching television when he suddenly made an announcement. He told his wife that one of the supporting pillars had only one vine leaf whilst the other had two. The fireplace was an expensive purchase and very subtle, almost invisible, vine leaves were carved into the structure. This revelation sent Martha into a spasm of letter writing from which she received many replies all of which meant the seller, refused to take any steps to rectify the problem. I came home from work one night and my wife handed me a file of voluminous proportions. It revealed documents drafted by Martha, the sellers, CAB and Trading Standards. After spending a few hours reading them and taking notes, it was clear that the sellers were not prepared to act. However, as I leafed through the company's catalogue, I noticed the advert for the fireplace included a photograph, which clearly showed both pillars had two vine leaves. I wrote to the company giving them fourteen days to respond. I pointed out that the photograph constituted a sale by description under the Sale and Supply of Goods Act and consequently they were liable. A week or so later the sellers arrived with a new pillar with two leaves and replaced the offending one. The moral of this tale for all husbands is if you notice something similar don't tell the wife.

Outside of work I had finally completed my application to the European Court of Human Rights. When you stripped away the arcane language it was basically saying that the British Government's Department of Health and Social Security was ignoring its own rules to deprive certain disabled people of a rightful benefit. It began:

'I John Keeman ... born in the country of Scotland respectfully apply for the determination of the European Court of Human Rights in the following matter which concerns the High Contracting Party the United Kingdom of Britain and Northern Ireland.'

The preliminaries went on to say that the UK Government had breached Articles 6 and 13 of the European Convention on Human Rights. That the applicant had exhausted all domestic remedies and the European Court should decide in favour of the applicant. It was a Bound Volume that finally found its way to Strasbourg. Months later a ruling arrived from the court finding on behalf of the Government. However, it contained a number of points that indicated the decision may have been a little different if certain action had been taken. We came close, but no cigar. In the letter that accompanied the decision it was stated that the decision was confidential between the parties which I found quite incredible and basically ignored. The following year the Human Rights Act, which so angers many Tories to this day, was introduced into the UK meaning people with a similar complaint could bring it before the British Courts and Tribunals.

145

Chapter Eleven

London Visits

In February 1999 I was back in London for a few days. I had not long booked into the Kennedy Thistle Hotel in Euston when I got a phone call from Neil Shaw, a former colleague who now worked with the BBC in London. We arranged to meet in a pub across from St. Pancras Station, where we had a discussion on introducing Interactive Voice Response (known as IVR) to the Helpline's telephone system. It was basically an up-market answering machine. The concept was to use an IVR for programmes that were expected to receive a high volume of calls. In fact, all television programmes eventually carried an IVR. We further agreed that setting up and recording IVRs would become the responsibility of the Research Team and we talked through the sort of training that would be needed. Later I remember recording IVRs in my local pub, at home and anywhere else where a phone was handy. On these occasions some television producer would have decided to trail our number without advance warning and if none of my team was available, I would get a call to the pub or my home to quickly set one up.

The day after my meeting with Neil I attended a 'Fairness at Work' seminar at a Hotel in the centre of London. It was a very informative day with a nice meal and a few drinks. The next morning, I had a hearty breakfast before getting a taxi from my hotel to the BBC's *Law in Action* studio for an arranged visit. I now wrote briefing sheets for that particular programme and was interested in seeing how it was made and it was not quite what I expected. When you listen to a discussion on a radio programme it is normal to assume that the presenter and guests are in the studio together. I was shown into a small studio and at the other side of a window the presenter sat alone with a tape recorder. He introduced his first guest, then asked a question, pushed a button on the tape and got an answer back. In fact, the whole programme went along these lines. Interviews had been pre-recorded outside the studio at a guest's home or place of work and I found it quite comical to watch the animated presenter carry on as if there was another person in the room when he was alone. I suppose for him it added some realism to the process. I made a point of listening to a recording of the broadcast and I couldn't see the join.

It was sometime during that week when I heard the term 'Millennium Bug' for the first time. This was the concept that due to the way computers were set as regards to dates, when we reached midnight on the 21st of December 2000, the machines would not function. According to so-called experts, banks, insurance companies and government institutions would cease to operate. Other doomsday predictions included planes falling out of the sky, train crashes, shipwrecks and a host of other disasters where computers were used. There was no shortage of experts appearing on radio and television to voice their opinion with little area of agreement between them as to what would happen. A bit like the current Brexit fiasco. Despite these prophets of doom, we moved without difficulty into the 21st Century, with many of the soothsayers claiming it was not the new millennium until January 2001.

My world chugged along much the same as usual, but I was now jointly managing a team of researchers along with Audrey who was a former Department of Social Security officer. Despite this we got along well together. It had been my idea for some time that the service would benefit from having a dedicated research team but on each occasion when I brought the subject up, it was quickly dismissed, and became

147

known as John's 'Dream Team.' It was never my nature to give up on something I believed in and I felt strongly that we could produce better quality information, avoid duplication, and form a better relationship with external agencies if we had a team of full-time researchers.

I was at my desk one morning when Audrey told me we were due at a meeting in a hotel around the corner from the offices. 'That's a management meeting. We're not managers. Why would we be required at this meeting?' I asked.

'I don't know,' she said. 'Charles said I was to be there and to bring you along.'

Charles was the CEO so it was like a command from God and I followed the messenger. At the meeting I got another chance to raise the issue of a dedicated research team and waited for the usual groans of derision. Instead a voice piped up.

'Go ahead,' it was Charles.

'You and Audrey assess what resources you need to set it up and let's go with it. Both of you come and see me when you have something to report.'

I was quite taken aback and surprised that my dream team was about to become a reality, and later a nightmare at times. Over the next few weeks Audrey and I spent hours working out how many staff we would need, the job advertisement, whether to require applicants to sit a written test, what hours they would need to work to meet the requirements of the business, what the salary should be, and a whole load of other issues. Finally, we settled on fifteen staff and advertised internally. We received a large number of applications and began to interview applicants with some trepidation. However, things went quite smoothly and during one interview, when a female applicant was advised there would be a written test, she asked if there would be any foreplay. The question threw me until my tiny brain worked out that she meant roleplay. I had never seen anyone's face go as red as hers until that day and not since. Needless to say, she passed the test and was selected.

With the team in place and training ongoing we occupied part of the library. With a bank of computers, individual telephones and desks we began the process of producing briefing sheets and feedback reports for programme makers. At the initial training I spoke with the team and advised that I intended to borrow some Marxist ideas to run the team. Karl Marx proposed, among other things, that once society had reached a certain level the State would wither away. My idea was that once the team had reached a certain level of competence, the management would hopefully wither away. Of course, they laughed at 'Red John', but in truth after a few months any one of them could have successfully managed the team.

Meanwhile I spent more time than I wanted to spare going to meetings that were at best unproductive, and at worst useless talking shops. Senior management were by this time steeped in the idea that every minor issue required a meeting to resolve it and on my return from holiday, I was faced with a series of emails referring to DORMS, WORMS and MORMS. When I enquired as to what they meant I was informed that they were Daily Operational Review Meetings, Weekly Operational Review Meetings and Monthly ... nine meetings a month, each one more pitiful than the last.

During the year the team produced information on a vast number of topics dealing largely with health and finance matters. The day of the Government's annual Budget was traditionally chaotic in the office. Researchers would listen to the Chancellor's speech and the analysis that followed, taking down as much information as possible to produce a briefing sheet. This would suffer a number of amendments as new information arrived, and the office printers worked overtime to keep up-to-date copies available to staff. On the day we normally engaged secondees with particular expertise in areas of taxation, national insurance, pensions and benefits. These usually came from an accountancy firm, Kidsons Impey, based downstairs. Their staff assisted Helpline workers with answers to the more complex enquiries. The day before the Budget I delivered training sessions on income tax, inheritance tax, capital gains tax, and VAT. It was very basic and designed simply to let telephone agents get accustomed to the jargon and be able to distinguish one tax from another. The Kidsons Impey staff really loved working with the Helpline. It was such a change from their normal job of moving figures about on a computer screen. Here they had no idea what sort of question they would be asked next and had very little time to form an answer. They could be asked how to avoid paying inheritance tax one minute and how much of an increase was put on a gallon of petrol the next. In fact, one of the accountants worked with the Helpline on Friday evenings because he enjoyed the change and often assisted me in producing a briefing sheet for Radio 4's *Moneybox* programme that went out on Saturday mornings.

During the year we continued to help support the Radio 4 Appeal. This is a weekly three-minute programme highlighting the work of a charity and appealing for donations. Charities can apply for an appeal to be read out on air and applications are assessed by a panel of external assessors and an advisory committee. The programme is broadcast on Sunday afternoons with a repeat during the week.

In March the BBC ran a campaign under the banner of: 'Make a Will Week.' A report suggested herbal cigarettes caused damage to health, another claimed trains loaded with nuclear waste were travelling through London and The Centre for Policy Studies claimed Britain was adopting a compensation culture with £8 billion being claimed that year. To coincide with this, newspapers and the BBC reported on a sex discrimination case where the claimant was awarded over thirty-eight thousand pounds. On the lighter side I was involved in researching a Radio 4 drama that celebrated the one-hundredth anniversary of Ruskin College in Oxford. I spoke with a number of Oxford dons and the Dean of Ruskin College, none of whom were the least bit pretentious or anything like the characters in *Inspector Morse*.

In April we were involved in the first election of a Scottish Parliament. Our remit was to explain the voting system to callers, advise them on the division of the one hundred and twenty-nine seats, and give general information on how the mixed-member proportional representation system operated. Information was provided by the Electoral Commission.

Around this time one of our Asian staff was subjected to verbal abuse from a couple of neds who were ejected from a bus on Sauchiehall Street outside our office, where she was waiting for her lift home. They began hurling abuse at her then ran off. I met her on the stairs as she made her way back to the office and she was extremely distraught. She told me what happened and I ran downstairs to see two policemen with the two boys in custody. I spoke with them and they later came to see the victim at our offices for a statement. Some weeks later she got a witness summons but said she was very reluctant to appear in court. I told her that lawyers will wait until they see if witnesses appear on the day. If they do the chances are they'll plead their clients guilty and she wouldn't be needed. I saw she was quite unconvinced by my advice so I offered to go with her to the court on the day. As I had suggested, the wee bastards did not turn up and a warrant was issued for their arrest. I presume they got arrested at some stage but we heard no more about it.

I'd appeared in court a few times in different capacities. I'd been an accused, a witness, a claimant and also a foreman on two juries. Being elected a foreman on a jury is not some special honour. The truth is no one wants to do it. On the first occasion after the jury was picked, we were taken to the jury room by a clerk who left us and went outside the door. Most of the jury hovered around the tea and coffee machines and after about ten minutes I suggested we should get on with things. Some of them said they were waiting for the clerk to come back in and when I said she was not allowed in the room while we were deliberating that was enough for me to be considered an expert and elected foreman. The second occasion was similar in that one of the jury asked if anyone had been on a jury before. I was the only one who had been, so I was selected again. It is of course illegal to discuss what went on inside the jury room but in the first case we found the accused innocent and in the second case guilty. Both cases involved assault charges and took the full week to resolve.

At work I had a call from a producer I had invited to the Helpline some weeks before. She was having an issue receiving her expenses and asked if I could get it sorted. I spoke with our accountant and her response led me to think we were not in as financially secure a position as we were being led to believe, which perhaps explained the restructuring, the loss of some jobs and replacing leavers with staff on the minimum wage.

It did not, at that point, look like the future was rosy.

BBC Radio Helpline

Chapter Twelve

The New Millennium

At midnight on the 31st of December 1999, planes did not fall out of the sky, nor did computers all around the world fail. The Millennium Bug was a washout. At the stroke of midnight, I was in my garden carrying our Yorkshire Terrier, Toby. Suddenly the sky lit up and fireworks went off all over the place, the dog was shaking and terrified until I found a quiet part of the house away from the noise. Eventually it all died away and we were in the New Millennium.

Restructuring was the buzzword at work, some staff were required to apply for their own jobs and there were rumours that staff were complaining of being bullied. In fact, someone reported this to the press and the *Sunday Mail* carried out an investigation. We also had a visit from an MP whom I spoke with and I advised him he could speak to any of my team on the premises or outside the building. His visit, in my view, was a waste of public money but it can be argued so much of what MPs do is the same.

The business was indeed changing and it was clear that there was a move to reduce the time spent on social action calls by simply offering a caller a referral to another agency. This did not sit well with a lot of staff, including my boss at the time, and she resigned later in the year. I got an invitation to her leaving party and a few staff reckoned when I went into her house it would likely fall down. She was a minister's wife and stayed in a manse.

Profit was now the main objective and all sorts of management tools were introduced to get as much work out of staff as possible: targets, key performance indicators, monthly appraisals; and a whole host of managerial jargon had entered the normal vocabulary. Staff were encouraged to be critical of their own performance during their appraisals, but I point-blank refused to criticise my own work. In one appraisal form I paraphrased Philip Larkin's poem: 'They Fuck You up Your Mum and Dad.'

They fuck you up your managers
They always mean to and they do
They fill you with their thoughts and fears
And then add extra just for you
But they were fucked up in their turn
By Harvard suits in cashmere coats
Who half the time was sober, stern
And half as drunk as winter stoats
Boss hands on misery to man
It deepens as a coastal shelf
Get out as early as you can
And tell them - go and fuck yourself

My appraiser asked me if she was to take this seriously and I told her Philip Larkin was offered the position of Poet Laureate in 1984, so they took him seriously enough. Of course she did not accept it. It was around this time I decided I would likely need the support of a trade union at some stage in the future so I joined BECTU - The Broadcasting, Entertainment, Cinematograph and Theatre Union, and the least said about them the better. Industrial relations were pretty poor and over the coming months some staff left, some raised grievance procedures, others joined a union and some people quite openly became management lackeys. It had gone from the best job I ever had to just a job.

A couple of my team had moved to another department and it was agreed I could replace them. However, I was advised by senior management that staff based in Ireland should be allowed to apply. I told them I thought this was absurd as the Research Team was based in Glasgow and all written programme information and reports were produced in that office. Moreover, how was I supposed to supervise someone's work when they were thirty-odd miles across the sea? In the event management stuck to their guns and about a dozen staff from Belfast applied. It was arranged that they would sit the test paper in Belfast and, if put on the short list, would come to Glasgow for the interview. I sent a copy of the test with answers attached to the manager who was supervising the test. A week or so later I had the test papers returned to me for marking and on reading the first paper I was very familiar with the answer to the first question. I had written it. The manager had photocopied the test paper and answer paper and distributed both to the applicants. Over three-quarters of them had simply copied out the answers which, in my opinion, was enough for them to fail.

In the end one applicant was given the job but it was an absurd situation. He was a member of a team who were all based over thirty miles away from his desk and he had to be emailed minutes of team meetings and other meetings. A lot of my time was wasted speaking to him on the phone or chasing him up for work that was needed quickly. I refused to go to Ireland to carry out his appraisals so he had to come to Glasgow once a month. In basic terms it was a bloody nonsense.

I was still involved with the *Watchdog* programme and in contact with the Director of the Institute of Trading Standards each week. The main *Watchdog* broadcast was on Wednesday evenings but it had a sister programme that went out on Friday nights. The Friday broadcast was a more light-hearted look at consumer issues. One Friday evening I was working a couple of hours late to finish a *Moneybox* brief for the Saturday broadcast. I'd had a look through the *Watchdog* script which revealed the programme was doing a piece on theatres in London that still displayed the original posters advertising the play. This meant the public could see a poster advertising, say, Albert Finney and Tom Courtney, but in fact they had left the play many years before. I was just about to leave the office when my telephone rang and at the other end I heard the voice of a well-known actor. He said he was starring in a play in London and had been watching *Watchdog* before he set off for the evening performance. He told me there was a shot of the theatre he was appearing in, and when his name appeared on the billboard the presenter made a remark about stars being replaced by mediocre actors.

'Can you advise the producers of this drivel that I do not consider myself a mediocre actor, neither does my agent or my fans,' he said. I advised him I could record it as an official complaint but he said an email to the producer was sufficient. I thought then, and still do, that he was having a laugh and was not playing the injured thespian.

Some weeks later he called me again, this time with a genuine enquiry. It was a Saturday afternoon and he said his chauffeur told him he heard an advert for the *Jimmy Young Show* on Radio 2 saying that he was due on the show the following Monday. The actor said he had no knowledge of this and neither had his agent. I advised there was nobody from the programme available on Saturdays but I would phone security in London and see what I could do. He left me his mobile number and I called him back later to tell him security at Portland Place had left a note in the programme studio. I had emailed and left answer machine messages for various producers of the programme. He thanked me and offered some tickets for the play, but I told him I was based in Glasgow. I could have made a few quid selling some of the female staff his mobile number when they heard the story about his call. In the event he did appear on the programme as a guest who was opposed to the traffic congestion charges being suggested in London at the time.

Speaking with quite famous people went with the job, but as they were calling a confidential helpline giving their names in these writings would be a breach of trust. I recall an actress phoned one day looking for information on a Radio 4 drama for her actor husband. She said he would have called himself but he was in Edinburgh for an audition. I was quite taken aback because this actor, in my opinion, was one of Britain's finest and I could not quite believe he would have to audition for anything. I managed to retrieve the information she was looking for but I never found out if he got the part.

When a newspaper item suggested that the BBC were negotiating to show a repeat of a six-part series first shown in 1987, I received a call from one of the original cast. Apparently, the show was never repeated, despite rave reviews from audiences, due to a copyright issue. I had to advise him that as far as I was aware the press item was simply speculation and the long-term schedules that I had access to did not indicate the programme was due for a repeat broadcast. The programme he referred to was *Tutti Fruiti*, and it has now been repeated.

Politicians were regular callers, with various enquiries and sometimes complaints about BBC being biased in favour of one party or another. The fact that these calls came from multiple parties was always enough for the BBC to claim that this meant there was no bias. One call I received from a member of the House of Lords was not about bias but about a white hat. The lady in question asked if the BBC had a photograph of her in her new white hat at Royal Ascot. I had to advise that as the BBC had filmed the racing, they likely did not send a stills photographer, and consequently there was no copy available. I suggested she try Reuters news agency but I also advised she could obtain a copy of the racing programme on a DVD and view it to see if she was picked up in the carriage behind the Queen. 'What's a DVD?' she asked. I explained what this technology involved but she

157

had no DVD player or indeed a television. I arranged for a DVD through Contributor Access that she said she could watch at a friend's house.

I had another enquiry from a member of the House of Lords in relation to the *Crimewatch* programme. The show had shown a variety of valuable items that had been recovered by the police following burglaries. They were trying to trace the owners and panned round the various pieces, paintings, silverware, pottery, furniture and so on. I received a call from a person who identified himself as Lord so-and-so. He said he thought he recognised a painting that may have been stolen from one of his houses, following a series of break-ins to his properties. I pondered on exactly how many houses he had, but said I would put the producer in touch with him and he left his private House of Lords number. Later I got a call from the producer saying she had spoken with him but the painting was not one of his. He phoned a further three times after programmes but the items he mentioned always turned out not to be his. On the last occasion I suggested to the producer that she should just give him something.

All of the well-known, if not exactly famous, people I spoke with were very polite, and mostly fans of the BBC. However, one particularly pretentious male actor got his underwear in a twist when I mispronounced his surname and he proceeded to spell it out using the phonetic alphabet. He then called me Keenan so I took the opportunity to follow his lead. I think he got the message.

Some programmes were difficult to support and often created problems for our staff, outside organisations and the audience. I remember late one Friday afternoon I received a call from a Director of the British School of Motoring. He told me the company's offices around the country were receiving enquiries from pensioners about a free driving test being offered, to assess whether they had picked up any bad habits over the years. He was sure, following his enquiries, that the issue began with something being said on a radio show and was demanding an explanation. I told him I would have to investigate and phone him back but he insisted he wanted an explanation that evening. I began by looking through the calls we'd had on radio that day and there seemed to be quite a number of enquiries related to the British School of Motoring. Eureka! I called him back and advised that the programme was the *Jimmy Young Show*, broadcast on Radio 2. I explained that it carried an item discussing whether people in their seventies should be subjected to a driving assessment to see if they were still fit to hold a licence. I also advised that I would need time to investigate where the story about free tests came from. Fortunately, this pacified him and he gave me a private number where he could be reached. I continued my enquiries over the weekend and by Monday afternoon I had his answer. He was not going to like it I was sure, but the reality was what it was.

I called him just after lunchtime and told him the programme took calls from listeners and broadcast them on-air. I also advised that a listener from Wales, who had been listening to the discussion about driving tests, called in, and said his local BSM shop offered free assessments for pensioners. This had encouraged listeners from all over the country to contact their local BSM.

'Are you telling me that the BBC broadcast that nonsense over the air without checking its authenticity?' he said, his voice filled with incredulity.

'As far as I can determine that's correct,' I said, adding, 'I can only apologise.'

'I've a good mind to send the BBC a bill for all the time myself and my staff spent on this wild goose chase initiated by the BBC's failure to check information before they broadcast it to all and sundry. Who should I send it to if I so decide?'

'You could try the BBC Accounts Department,' I said. 'I can give you contact details for them but I would be inclined to contact the producer and send the bill to him. I'll just get his email address for you.'

It was a ridiculous mistake to make. Of course, one of the programmer researchers should have checked out the information before allowing it to be broadcast over the air, but people are human and make mistakes. Even those who work at the BBC, as Cliff Richard would confirm many years later.

The New Year began with the resignation of our Director, who had not been heard from since early December. At a series of meetings, a temporary replacement told staff everything was okay, jobs were safe and people should not be concerned. No reason was ever given for the resignation and when directly asked the temporary boss went into management fudge mode. A new phone-room manager was appointed on a sort of consultancy basis and a whole new vocabulary of management speak was born. I had many meetings with her, all of which I found consisted of incoherent drivel.

I began to suffer severe pain in my shoulder and following a number of visits to my doctor with no relief, I dabbled in acupuncture. The clinic was in an old mansion house just outside Troon, with wood-panelled walls, coal fires and leather armchairs and sofas. The receptionist, a pleasant, matronly type, sat at a highly-polished old wooden table and asked me for some very brief details. After I'd completed the form I was invited to sit down and did so on a very comfortable armchair next to a coal fire and watched all the bad backs, dodgy hip joints and arthritic knees go for treatment. Most of them returned looking none the worse for wear. Almost exactly on the appointed time a small man in his late forties to early fifties appeared and invited me into a consulting room that looked something like a Victorian study with bookshelves, display cases, two large leather sofas and a large desk. He asked what my problem was and I gave brief details of what my doctor had said, to which he replied with one word – treatment. A female assistant asked if I'd had acupuncture before and I thought of saying I hadn't and I wasn't having it now either, but it came out as a simple 'no.' She then attached the needles to a machine not unlike a car battery charger with four wires, two yellow, one red and one blue. When she turned it on, a series of small impulses ran down my neck along my shoulders and down my left arm. The sensation was neither painful nor pleasurable and for the next twenty minutes or so I sat on the stool with my shoulders looking like a pin cushion and read a newspaper, that I had spread out on the bed facing me. Every now and then I would have a look at the machine and wonder - what wire should I cut? I could, of course, just have flicked the switch to the off-position. The small man and his assistant came back into the cubicle. She removed the needles and wiped my shoulders with some liquid that stung a bit like a cheap aftershave. I paid for my treatment at the matron's desk, made my next appointment and left. When I got to the bottom of the driveway I leaned on the gate, lit a cigarette and the pain had gone, but it was a short-lived relief.

The pain was finally diagnosed by conventional doctors as cervical spondylitis and I was referred to physiotherapy. On my first visit, I was sitting in the waiting room when this very tall black man, who looked like Little Richard, appeared from a room opposite. He called my name in a booming voice and suddenly I felt a bit better. He showed me into a room that was very sparsely furnished with two straight back chairs, a desk and an examination table.

'So why are you here?' he asked.

'My doctor says I have cervical spondylitis,' I answered.

'I don't care what your doctor said. I asked you why are you here?'

I tried to work out what he expected me to say so I just said that I had a very painful shoulder. I didn't like taking painkillers and I'd tried acupuncture but it didn't work.

'That's right,' he said. 'You are here because you are in pain.'

At this time, I was standing in the middle of the room while he was seated on one of the chairs, the other being hard against a wall. He ordered me to remove my jacket and shirt, rose from the chair and walked around me.

'You have the worst posture I have ever seen,' he said, 'can you tell me why?'

By this time, I was pissed off with him. 'I drove trucks and humped tons of stuff every day for over twenty years, maybe that's got something to do with it,' I said, irritated.

'Lie down with the back of your head resting on the floor, keep your arms and legs straight. Do not bend your knees or elbows. Do that for ten minutes a few times during the day and just before you get into bed.'

I thought he was nuts, but I'd tried everything else so I gave it a go. After a week or so the pain began to ease and I felt there was more movement in my neck. I saw him every two weeks and we became quite chatty. He told me he came from Kenya and suffered badly from back pain as a young man. He arrived in London to study medicine but chose to concentrate on the relationship between muscles and bones, to the point where he became a leading expert on the subject. About two months after following his advice I lost a good deal of weight, could almost turn my head three hundred and sixty degrees and the pain was gone. What a guy!

Work was the source of another type of pain usually around the nether regions. Restructuring continued apace with new job titles being created and some people appointed to positions that were not advertised, which caused even more disquiet. My research team did not escape with my co-manager being seconded to another department. To replace her I was permitted to advertise for a team leader and it came down to two applicants. Two managers on the interview panel selected the same applicant but I pointed out it was me who would work with the successful candidate and I chose the other. In the end it was the correct decision and she made a very good team leader. The other candidate left soon after to become a private detective with a Glasgow firm called the Criminal Investigation Agency or CIA - you cannot make this stuff up.

Around the middle of the year a group from the Consumers Association in London visited our offices and I was charged with giving them the tour. They were very impressed as to how quickly staff could react to trails on radio and television and invited me to visit their offices in London. I was more than happy to accept, but there was bad news awaiting when I came home after that particular trip.

On Thursday the 4th of November 2001 I was on my way home from London and I phoned Janet from Crewe to tell her the trains were running hours late due to reduced speed limits following severe flooding. She had bad news. A few hours earlier she had gone upstairs to see our son John and found him standing in the middle of his room unable to move. He was rigid and was clutching a bottle of cola in his hand and he also had difficulty speaking. She immediately called the mental health team and an ambulance was called. Meanwhile Janet and our son Stephen managed to get him downstairs to await the ambulance. When the ambulance crew arrived and saw John's condition they called for a GP. Two doctors arrived but neither had any thought of what was wrong and had John admitted to hospital. The psychiatrist who examined him in hospital said she had never seen a patient present with such symptoms before.

I arrived home in the early hours of the morning and after a short sleep I visited the hospital. John was on a number of monitoring machines; he had muscular rigidity, could not speak, was drooling, and had a very high temperature and high blood pressure. He did not recognise me and appeared extremely ill. At that moment, I feared for his life. The doctors who had examined him so far were unable to diagnose what the problem was. The particular doctor I was speaking with asked if he could have taken an overdose, but I had asked Janet this and she had checked his medication and what should have been there, was there. The doctor then asked if he could have taken any other drugs, by which I reckoned she meant illegal substances. I also reassured her that he hadn't and the conversation turned to poisons. I immediately went home and checked all the kitchen cleaning materials, bleach, disinfectants and so on but everything seemed as it should be. I called the hospital and advised that after a count of John's medication, and a complete search of his room, I could find nothing that would explain his condition.

Over the weekend his condition remained the same. Doctors worked on reducing his fever, blood pressure and temperature. He was seen by a number of specialists including a German toxicologist who also said he had never seen someone exhibit such symptoms before but he opined it was likely that it was related to his anti-psychotic medication.

I returned to work after the weekend and carried out some research on John's medication. On reading about the drug Clozaril (Clozapine) I came across a very rare medical condition named Neuropleptic Malignant Syndrome. Every symptom that John had - tremors, muscle rigidity, high temperature, and so on - was present in sufferers of NMS. When I researched the treatment, it was much the same as John was receiving: try to reduce temperature, blood pressure, fever, and medicate with antibiotics. The hospital doctors were doing this and more, although they still had not put a name to his illness. It was a comfort to know they were on the right track and I was more hopeful than earlier.

Over the coming week John was very ill. He was deeply depressed, suffering a great deal of pain and withdrawn. He had a catheter fitted, and often refused food and medication. Inevitably I was asked for permission to have him sectioned under the Mental Health Acts. I did not want to do this but I realised it was perhaps the only way he was ever going to get well, so I agreed. At one point he was given Electro Convulsive Therapy but it did not really improve his well-being. Following a change in his medication he began to recover from the NMS and eventually he got home. His mental health remains a concern to this day but he is still at home with his family. His brother Stephen is his carer nowadays, and they get on well together but not all the time, just like brothers the world o'er. NMS is a reaction in some patients to the anti-psychotic drug Clozaril. At that time, it was manufactured by Sandoz, and they had some success in treating schizophrenic patients. However, it had one major drawback in some cases - it stopped the body from producing white blood cells meaning even a minor infection could be fatal. In John's case he could no longer be treated with this particular drug. He did make a full recovery from NMS and a few years later his doctors suggested they try him on Clozaril again, this time under strict monitoring by Sandoz. Almost immediately he began showing the early symptoms of NMS and it was stopped.

I considered legal action against Sandoz on the grounds that neither John nor his carers were advised of the dangers when he was first prescribed Clozaril. If we had been aware of the possibility that John would become so ill that he would have to learn to speak and walk all over again I doubt if we would have consented at the time. After all there were other anti-psychotic drugs around that did not carry such a risk. But we can all show wisdom after the event. I spoke with lawyers both in Scotland and in the United States and voluminous correspondence flew between them and Sandoz, but in the end, it would have been very expensive and also very difficult to prove fault, which is essential under our judicial system and also to prove negligence against another legal entity. Moreover, John's mother did not want him to

have to relive the horrible time he had in hospital and I came
to agree. Compassion overcame compensation and we got on
with our lives.

Anderston Library

Chapter Thirteen

Sixty-Two Thousand Calls

At the beginning of 2002 I was considering looking for other work but I thought at 58 years old, very few, if any, employers would be interested. I could always get part-time work on taxis and ice cream vans, but I did not want to return to people complaining about too many black wine gums in a mix-up or drunks who could not remember where they stayed. I considered setting up a consultancy where I would offer small businesses advice and information on how to avoid being taken to an Employment Tribunal. I went as far as delivering a presentation on tribunals to a group of self-employed household removers at their Furniture Association's annual dinner. It was an interesting evening and afterwards I spoke with many of the guests. Many of them had horror stories of having to pay disgruntled employees because it was cheaper than paying a lawyer to defend them. Following some further research, mostly into what finance and resources I would need, it became clear my future did not lie in the consultancy business. Fortunately, my enthusiasm for my job was re-kindled when my team were asked to support and episode of *Panorama* entitled 'The Secrets of Seroxat.'

Seroxat was among the world's biggest selling and most successful anti-depressants, but the programme alleged the drug was addictive and some people suffered serious withdrawal symptoms when they tried to stop. It further alleged that taking the drug could lead to some people self-harming or taking their own lives and there was little warning of these possible side effects. The manufacturer denied these allegations but the programme had support from leading experts on the drug, who had access to confidential Seroxat studies in the manufacturer's archives. The programme followed one Seroxat user as she went through a nine-month struggle to wean herself off the drug. The BBC were in this instance taking on one of the largest and most powerful drug manufacturers in the world and any information we passed on to the public had to be up-to-date and accurate. The morning after the programme aired, I got a call from the reporter who also presented the programme.

'Did we get many calls after last night's broadcast, John?' She asked. I gave her the latest figure I had.

'Sixty-two thousand and they're still coming in,' I told her. I also said we would send a feedback report later in the day and keep her up to date over the next week or so until the calls died away. The public response to the broadcast was such that *Panorama* made another three documentaries about Seroxat, which was a major change in the programme's policy of only visiting a subject once.

Some weeks after the *Panorama* broadcast the BBC ran a domestic violence campaign, entitled *Hitting Home*. Storylines, featuring scenes of domestic violence, were shown in *Casualty*, *Neighbours*, *EastEnders* and in a powerful documentary *Dangerous Love*. These attracted a large number of calls, some of which were complaints about the Christmas Day edition of *EastEnders* for containing 'disturbing' scenes of domestic violence. In fact, the Broadcasting Standards Commission strongly criticised the BBC following complaints from the public. Weeks after the conclusion of the Campaign, BBC *EastEnders'* producers toured the country speaking with groups of people involved in helping victims of domestic violence. I was invited to one of these evenings in the Glasgow Film Theatre, along with my boss, who was on the panel assembled on stage. After numerous questions from the audience, we went for a drink with an *Eastenders*' producer and during the conversation he said he was staying overnight and visiting the *River City* site the next day.

'Do you know why the location for the programme is called Shieldinch?' I asked and he said he didn't.

I told him that on the north side of the River Clyde was an area known as Whiteinch and on the other side an area known as Shieldhall. The location could easily have been called Whitehall, I said.

These programmes generated some hope in staff that the social action remit was not all lost, but we were now joined with BBC information that had moved from London to Belfast and in Glasgow we hosted the correspondence unit who replied to written letters to the BBC on almost any topic in the world. A team leader, who previously worked in the phone room, gave me a letter that she thought I might like. It was hand-written on expensive paper with a little coloured motif of a cottage across the top. It was from a doctor and postmarked Kingston-Upon-Thames. The subject of the letter was a demand for the BBC to push for a public holiday on the Queen Mother's one-hundredth birthday. It went on in this vein and I wondered why my colleague thought I would be interested in the royalist rant until I got to the last paragraph which went:

'I think the Queen Mother's one-hundredth birthday should be celebrated by a public holiday so that we can all do what the Royal Family have been doing for years: Fuck All.'

There were various changes at work around this time and eventually I had to sign a new contract with the new masters. I held off as long as I could, as did many of my team, but when push came to shove, we had no legal argument for retaining our old BBC contracts.

I was seated at my desk one Friday afternoon when a director and my boss came into the phone room, both walking with purpose. They headed straight for my desk and when they got there the director proceeded to shut down my computer. My boss told me I was suspended and had to leave the building. I've always found it better to comply with this kind of melodramatic approach by some managers and deal with it when you get the official reasons for their actions in writing, so I left.

I went to my local pub in Hope Street for a beer and met with a few of my mates who worked in the city and finished early on Fridays. I was sitting having a drink with them and relating what had happened when my mobile phone rang. It was my boss telling me I could come back into work. I told her I was now acting in the capacity of a private individual and she could fuck off and hung up. She called back again and I told her she had no idea what she was doing and to put everything in writing and send it to my home. I also advised her I would not be returning to work until she did so, and she should not phone me again or I'd have her for harassment. When I hung up my mates were in hysterics. I had long dealt with jumped-up little pricks like her and the director, and there was nothing to fear from this pair of drama queens.

A letter duly arrived and I went to a meeting where they alleged that I had left an email that I had sent to a member of staff in the printer. The problem, as they saw it, was the member of staff was off sick and managers were not permitted to contact them in such circumstances. Frankly, I had never heard such rubbish and when I asked who found the email, they refused to tell me. The problem with what they were saying was that the email was a personal contact between me and a dear friend, who remains so to this day. It could not be construed in any way, shape or form, as harassing an employee who was off sick. It was all nonsense and another example of how managers tried to bully staff they did not like or agree with.

In the end I was given a written warning for the misuse

of company property, which I tore up and threw in the bin at my desk when my boss handed it to me. Following this drama my friends and colleagues wondered what awful crime I had committed that required such drastic intervention. But the director who closed down my computer would soon get himself into hot water through an email.

The whole episode was another example of being managed by someone who was not up to the job. Early in her career she had tried to encourage other team leaders to keep private files on each of their individual team members. I had the opportunity to tell her what I thought of this preposterous nonsense and the team leaders ignored her advice. It was a difficult relationship and I had an interview with her boss to tell her I was sick of my manager trying to undermine my position by going over my head when she could. However, she and her manager were chips off the old block and my complaints got nowhere. The email episode was her way of trying to get at me but it never worked.

She tried similar stunts with other staff including a friend of mine who eventually went off sick with stress. She also had the audacity to ask me to act as her witness in a disciplinary hearing against a colleague. I was delighted to refuse and tell her I was actually coming to the hearing in the capacity as my colleague's representative. I was not very popular at this time with management but I could do without their blessing. I had a good relationship with programme makers and the BBC representative who oversaw the whole social action project. I had a meeting with him about the way things were developing and he promised he would intervene if I asked him to do so. He was a gentleman and it was easy to see he had more influence and power with the BBC than any of our existing management.

One morning I got a call from my line manager saying she had a lady on the telephone complaining about the BBC *Action Line*. As my manager she should have taken the complaint herself but insisted I deal with it. The lady on the phone told me she had just returned from holiday and struggled to get her front door opened due to the number of letters behind it. On reading through them later, she concluded that most of the writers had obtained her address from the BBC. I assured her I would investigate her complaint and call her back. It was indeed our fault as a member of my team, who could not get the complainant on the phone, assumed it would be okay to use the address. Unfortunately, the address of her charity was also her private residence. I also carried out some internet research on the lady and her charity and found her one very interesting person. She had been searching for her GI father for fourteen years. She knew he was an American billeted in the UK during the Second World War, who had met her mother and the relationship produced a daughter. She formed her own charity and wrote a book about her search that helped 'war babies' to trace their American fathers.

American government agencies, using a confidentiality argument, had refused to provide any details on her father for years until her charity raised a law suit in the American courts. In the end the court case led to the development of a Freedom of Information Law in the United States, when the court found for the charity. She was finally reunited with her father in a happy meeting after all those years. I figured someone with this background would not think twice about suing the BBC, which she had threatened when she spoke with my boss. I decided there was nothing else to do but admit fault and offer an apology. I called her that evening and simply said that we had screwed-up. We failed to follow our own policy and simply assumed it would be okay. I advised I'd had a meeting with the research team and emphasised the importance of contacting organisations and individuals before giving out their details. I waited for an onslaught that never came.

'If you're telling me the BBC is taking responsibility for this, I'm happy to accept your apology but if it happens again, I will take legal action.'

Her threat of future legal action if we screwed up was said in a manner that told me it was not an idle one.

We then had a discussion about the difficulties experienced by those trying to trace their fathers and she promised to send details for our briefing sheet which she did a few days later. She was a very pleasant lady to speak with but I would not have liked taking her on in a legal debate. It must have been extremely frustrating to know that some government lackey knows where your father resides but won't tell you. Why could they not have written to these men for permission to pass on their details? There is a well-known saying that power corrupts and absolute power corrupts absolutely.

The BBC was going digital and we were providing information on set top boxes and other details. The adverts on television suggested that all you had to do was buy a box, plug it in and hey presto, hundreds of channels. I did not buy this and spoke with some experts and in fact they said most people would probably need a new aerial. We had a visit from a BBC manager to enlighten us on digital issues and she came to talk with me about my team's input to the information. At one point I suggested that the BBC advert could be viewed as misleading in that it made no reference to reception issues or otherwise. She assured me that she had considered this and felt the advert was perfectly legal. I said we would just have to agree to disagree on the legalities.

After she left, I was advised she was Jeremy Paxman's sister and an English barrister, but I must say she took it all in good sport.

Chapter Fourteen

Taking up Golf

On the personal front, John had fully recovered from the Neuroleptic Malignant Syndrome, but he was in and out of hospital, as his doctors sought a drug regime that would stabilise his moods. Janet was working in a factory that produced computer cables in Irvine. It was an American-owned business and their employment relations were founded in the dark ages. Unlike me, however, Janet just got on with things.

I sailed over to Ireland on a Sunday evening to deliver an induction course to new staff that had joined BBC Information at Blackstaff House. The journey from Troon across to Belfast was most pleasant and, after I booked into the Holiday Inn, I went for a walk around the town. It was so changed from what I had experienced in the 1970s. The barbed wire was gone as were the soldiers with guns and I could now appreciate what a lovely city Belfast was. I have never been back since but I hope to visit the city again before I shuffle off this mortal coil.

Back in Glasgow three of my workmates were organising a game of golf for the following Sunday at Troon. I had never played golf before but I'd played pitch and putt, so when I was asked if I wanted to make a foursome, I agreed. Shortly afterwards emails began to appear saying I was having my first game of golf and inviting staff to join a sweepstake by guessing what my score would be. Some of the numbers were, in my view, ridiculous and those who picked scores in the two-hundreds clearly knew less than me about golf.

On the Sunday I was picked up from my home in Irvine and driven to Troon. Willie, the organiser, produced a set of clubs I could use and we teed off. When we reached the eleventh or twelfth hole I was doing okay. I wasn't ready for the Open Championship, but doing all right.

My mobile rang and the voice at the other end identified himself as a BBC Producer attached to the *Panorama* programme. I asked how I could help and he said he was not happy with the briefing sheet my team had produced for that evening's broadcast. He was not very specific as to the problem and I got a bit irritated and told him I was playing golf and I would phone him later. Whatever the problem, there was plenty of time to resolve it, even if I had to travel to Glasgow with Willie. I could not imagine what the issue was as I had edited the brief on the Saturday afternoon and put it into the database. Only I and the research team had access to the database and none of them worked that weekend so it could not have been changed since I loaded it into the system.

I was unsure about the call so I phoned our office and spoke with Frank, the shift leader that afternoon. I gave him the name of the guy who had called me and asked him to check the database and find out exactly who he was. Frank agreed, said he would call me back, and asked how the golf was going. Soon after when he phoned, he told me the guy I'd spoken with was a senior producer with *Panorama*. With Frank having confirmed the guy's status I asked Willie if he would drop me at the office after our game was over, he agreed and suggested we got on with the game. Over the last few holes, with my mind trying to figure out the telephone call, I was hitting the ball all over the shop. Willie and Paul were standing near one of the greens as Ray lined up for his putt and I was a few yards behind them. I thought I heard Willie say,

'I think we should tell him now.'

It became clear they were talking about me so I walked

over and asked them what it was I should be told. Willie laughed as he told me the whole *Panorama* thing was a wind-up.

'The guy who phoned is a new start in the phone room and we picked him because we knew you wouldn't recognise his voice. Paul said you would probably be suspicious and likely to check with the office, so Frank was in on it as well.'

The three of them had a good laugh at my expense. I argued that they should take at least six shots off my score but they were not for having that and it was logged as a hundred and two. Decent pals would have at least put it below the ton.

We were on the golf course again the following Sunday, this time at a course in Dalmuir, near where Willie stayed in Drumchapel. The course was a series of hills and I expected Sherpa Tensing to turn up with a large St. Bernard carrying a cask of brandy. I was only weeks away from my sixtieth birthday and by the time we got to the last hole I thought I'd never reach it. It took us hours to get round and when we arrived at Willie's house, the Euro Cup Final between Greece and Portugal was about to start.

Willie had laid on pies and beer so we settled down to watch the match. As the teams emerged from the tunnel, the English commentator remarked that the Portuguese team were wearing the same colour shirts that England wore in the 1966 World Cup final. There was no reason whatsoever to mention England, they were not playing; the game was not a World Cup match and the two teams were Greece and Portugal. The producer should have had his arse kicked.

Sadly, one of our former colleagues at Helpline, or *Action Line* as it came to be known, took his own life. He was a former captain in the British Army before he joined Helpline and had completed many tours of Northern Ireland at the height of The Troubles. He was an excellent team leader and had a great sense of humour, being one of the founders of *The Stun* magazine. But at some point, he developed mental health issues and his death was a consequence of these. The funeral was a very sad affair held in a church in Kilmacolm. There was a large turnout including many of his former comrades.

He is the third young man I've been friends with who has committed suicide. One was found dead at the bottom of a cliff in America and the other threw himself in front of a train in Ayrshire. Although when I went through a depression as a young man myself and often felt I would be better off dead, I never really seriously considered suicide. I often thought of it briefly, but that was as far as it went. I miss these three guys, two of whom were great workmates and friends and the other a good friend I'd known since he was a teenager.

Back at work I was part of the great meetings bonanza. I once worked it out that I was attending around a hundred meetings a month. At an average time of one hour this came to the equivalent of one fortnight each month sitting in meetings. I attended meetings every week with the eight individual team members. I carried out daily briefings with phone room staff. I went to operational reviews and management meetings. When the opportunity arose, we had video conferences with BBC staff in London and a physical meeting with BBC Scotland staff every Friday. My boss used to drag me along to these Glasgow meetings, although I rarely had any input to the agenda. Neither did a senior BBC Engineer who attended. The two of us used to chat among ourselves whilst the hierarchy got down to business.

One day he told me a story about a burial he attended on the east coast of Fife. The church was located very close to the North Sea and the deceased was a retired army colonel. The weather was horrendous that day and the mourners were lashed with rain as they stood at the graveside whilst the loquacious minister droned on. The engineer looked down into the grave and the coffin was beginning to float with the tide coming in. Suddenly, he heard a male mourner say, 'He's a retired army colonel and if the minister doesn't get a move on, he'll be buried at sea as if he was a retired Admiral.'

On the 28th of April 2004 I left the office early in the evening and headed for my favourite watering hole in Hope Street - the Pot Still - along with my colleague and friend, Ray. He bought a couple of pints and we sat in a corner facing the door. Within minutes of taking our seats, members of my research team started arriving. Ray had organised a surprise birthday party with free booze and food on the agenda. An hour or so later the party was in full swing when I noticed one of my former law lecturers standing at the bar. I assumed he had just finished an evening class at the University and was catching a refreshment on his way to the station. I walked over to see him and he turned round to greet me.

'I hear some old codger is having a party in here tonight. Happy Birthday!' he said.

My drinking buddy, Ray, had called the University and asked if they would send someone to represent my *alma mater*. He had also phoned my wife and asked if she had anything arranged for my birthday. Janet said she did not and I wasn't one for celebrating birthdays anyway and told him I would probably just go for a pint after work as usual. She was indeed right again. It turned out to be a splendid evening and I staggered on to the last train home laden with cards and presents. I can't remember if I appeared at work the following day.

The BBC *Action Line* provided information to a raft of BBC television channels, five national and over forty local radio stations. I recall one of local stations gave rise to a major complaint from the police. The presenter introduced an item about the police stopping people who were seen eating while driving their cars. One listener phoned in to say he had seen a woman police officer eating an apple when driving a police car. The presenter, in a moment of madness, commented along the lines that you would expect to see a pig with an apple in its mouth. Our telephones rang for a couple of hours after this including calls from serving policemen from all ranks including a chief constable. On another occasion a guest used the 'N' word on Radio 4 and calls went through the roof. There used to be a thing called the eight-second-delay which was to allow editing of these sorts of remarks but I don't know exactly how it worked. Obviously, it didn't on those two occasions.

As a consequence of one of my frequent management meetings, the research team were given the task of dealing with a part of the BBC known as Contributor Access. This department dealt with requests for copies or clips of programmes from people who had made a substantial contribution to a broadcast. There is a charge for the service and clips are not available if a person has simply been in the audience or had his mug shot shown on television at a football match or other event. Our remit was to provide information on completing an application form and the cost of a DVD or tape, to advise the criteria of a 'substantial contribution,' and to deal with enquiries and complaints. I took on the job of dealing with complaints about the service. I spoke most days with a BBC employee in London, who was very experienced in resourcing BBC Archives material. Once I got to know her quite well, I asked her if she could tell me how many copies of the 1966 World Cup Final the BBC actually had.

'Why?' she asked.

'Because no matter how many times it is shown it never seems to fade,' I told her.

'Enough,' she said.

One enquiry I dealt with early on was from a woman in London whose son suffered from a rare illness from which he was not expected to recover. He had been ill throughout his childhood and was one of a group of children who were part of a BBC documentary and taken to America for a holiday where it was filmed. She had completed an application form for a copy of her son's part of the documentary but had not received it and the boy's condition had so deteriorated he was expected to survive for only a few days. I called the BBC and after explaining the situation they contacted the Archives and they agreed to make the copy immediately and send it by special courier. I called to give his mother the news and she was quite overcome. A few days after the funeral she sent a card thanking us for getting the DVD on time and saying she would always remember the look on her son's face as he watched himself as a very young boy on television. It was so kind of her to remember other people in her terrible grief.

But this job had happier moments and one in particular that I enjoyed very much indeed. I got a call from a man who said he had applied for a clip from a documentary his father was mentioned in but was told he could not have it. The piece he was looking for came from a documentary televised in 1969 called *Royal Family*. The clip the applicant sought was of the Queen signing awards during which she mentioned the applicant's father by name and signed his citation for the Empire Medal he was soon to receive. His father had since died and his son was organising a memorial service during which he wanted to play the clip.

The BBC told him that the documentary was locked in the BBC vault by order of Her Majesty and was not to be shown again. There were a number of reasons why this decision was taken, among them was the view that it was too intrusive, and some said it made the Royal Family look too ordinary, particularly when it revealed the Queen used Tupperware tubs to store food. The applicant had various emails from Contributor Access refusing to consider his request and he called the Helpline to see if there was anything we could do. It looked unlikely, but I called the BBC and they confirmed that the documentary was stored in a vault and was not for public consumption. I called the applicant back with the bad news and he was extremely annoyed. He stated over and over again that he only wanted a clip of the few seconds when the Queen mentioned his dad's name and medal, and thought the decision was nonsense. I have to say I agreed with him but it looked as if nothing could be done. We continued having a conversation and it came to me that perhaps his next move should be to contact Buckingham Palace directly, explain the problem and ask for their help. I suggested he make his letter as brief as possible, avoid criticizing the BBC, concentrate on the reasons his dad was awarded the medal, and why he was seeking the clip. He immediately agreed to try this and said he would let me know what happened.

On the 13ᵗʰ of July 2005, he called me.

'I've to get it,' he shouted down the phone. 'I've got a letter from Buckingham Palace this morning from the Queen's Press Secretary, I've to get it. The Queen has granted permission, expressed her condolences and thanked my father for his contribution. Give me your fax number and I'll fax you a copy.'

He did and I still have it to this day. The bit I liked best in the letter was the paragraph where the secretary said,

'Please feel free to refer the BBC to me, if this letter does not suffice as authorisation to release the requested footage...'

After he hung up, I immediately called the BBC. Before I could say anything, they said,

'I know, I know, a researcher is pulling it out to copy as we speak, it will be sent off today.'

'It pays to have friends in high places, eh?' I said.

To this day the documentary has still not been shown again although some believe it will be, after the Queen has passed on. I later researched why the applicant's Flight Sergeant father was awarded The British Empire Medal and it transpired that he and others had went to the assistance of a Greek merchant ship, MV Daphne, that had caught fire. The ship was loaded with a dangerous cargo and the RAF Fire Service fought through the night in shark-infested waters to bring the fire under control. By daylight, under the command of the Flight Sergeant, they had succeeded but the ship's hold was full of water and there was a danger she would list and sink. The Flight Sergeant organised for pumps to be hauled aboard and many hours later the danger of sinking had passed. The firemen had spent three nights and two days aboard the Daphne with little sleep or food.

Contributor Access was a very interesting part of my job and the requests were varied, from people who had made quite a substantial appearance on television to those who had been fleetingly filmed dancing on *Top of the Pops* - applications for the latter were almost always unsuccessful.

Sometime in 2005 two of my closest friends and colleagues were, in my view, being treated rather badly at work and had been off sick for weeks. Before a female colleague went absent, she had been subject to some spurious disciplinary procedures, invited to meetings with little or no notice, and denied some basic rights - such as the right to have a witness present at meetings with management. She inevitably went off sick and began to receive letters and emails from management, many of which suggested her position was in jeopardy. Despite her using the company's grievance procedures, little was done to resolve the problem so she continued to be absent due to stress. As her former manager and friend, she asked if I could help and I agreed and suggested we meet outside work in the Pot Still. I began our meeting by asking her to explain what she wanted to achieve: Did she want an admission and apology by senior management that she was being treated badly? Did she want a move to another team? Did she want to give up her job and sue for compensation? Her response was immediate - she wanted out but did not want to leave with nothing.

I advised that there were two ways of perhaps achieving compensation for the loss of her job. Firstly, she could resign and submit a claim to an Employment Tribunal for constructive dismissal or secondly, she could stick it out by remaining on the sick until they fired her. The latter I advised would take months but I thought it was a better option. If an employer dismisses an employee, they have to satisfy a tribunal that the dismissal was fair and reasonable in all the circumstances. On the other hand, if an employee claims constructive dismissal, they have to satisfy a tribunal that the employer had breached the employee's contract to such an extent as to permit the employee to resign and claim compensation. It is a complicated procedure and best left alone in my view.

I was also concerned that her doctor kept using the word 'stress' on her absence certificates and suggested she ask him to use some other more meaningful term like depressive illness. Stress was not recognised by the World Health Organisation at that time as a specific illness and was more or less a buzzword that covered anything you wanted it to cover. In the end she agreed to stick it out and remained absent from work. She enlisted the help of her union representative, and I continued to read and respond to any correspondence emanating from management and union. The Union's position throughout was that she should accept any offer made.

After many months of shadow-boxing she received a letter inviting her to a meeting with the director. As the director was the only person who could dismiss her it was clear to me that the time had come. I met her in Starbucks on Sauchiehall Street before she went into the meeting, which was arranged outside her place of work at one of the company's offices in the town. I presumed this was to keep the dastardly deed as quiet as possible but it was just another symptom of management paranoia. I must say she looked better than she had in a while and was quite upbeat about things.

'You'll get fired this morning,' I said.

'I hope you're right,' she replied.

'I'll be back at the office,' I said, 'phone me when you are finished and we'll meet in Costa and you can tell me what happened.'

Less than an hour later I got her call. I told my team I was going out for a break and went over to Costa on Sauchiehall Street. She was already there when I went in and, on seeing me, she beamed from ear to ear. I knew at once she'd been dismissed and I thought I'd never seen anyone look so happy on losing their job. She explained that the meeting had been very short and the director asked her if she could provide a date for her return to work. She replied she could not and he proceeded to advise her that he would have to terminate her employment as she had lost the capacity to meet with the terms and conditions of her contract. The usual bullshit followed about the company being sorry it had come to this and how they were sorry to lose her and so on.

'Now comes the difficult bit,' I said. 'How do we get the bastards to come up with some decent compensation?'

Her dismissal generated a series of letters all on the same vein. The dismissal was not fair and reasonable in all the circumstances, the company should have considered alternative employment, and failing a reasonable offer we would raise a claim at the Employment Tribunal. The company's policy to date, going by other dismissals or resignations, was to settle and avoid any adverse publicity at tribunals. I was sure they would make an offer but the question was, would it be enough? My colleague had plans for her future and wanted to train as a teacher. She was in her early thirties and perfectly capable of achieving her aim if she had the financial assets. This presented me with a target figure which I never revealed, but I continued to reject a series of offers that I said were derisory. Eventually I prepared papers for the tribunal and had the case registered, I must admit with a certain amount of worry. The case was far from airtight on our part and I'd seen stronger cases fail. I was also concerned that she had taken the decision to trust my judgment without question and go against the views of her shop steward and union lawyer when I disagreed with their interpretation of the case. I would have collapsed in a heap if we lost after refusing a series of offers. Another offer was made and it was quite an increase from the previous. I was still inclined to reject it and I knew she would do so if I advised her so. I decided that we should arrange an appointment with her union lawyer and I would go with her. We would ask the lawyer if she would represent her at the tribunal if she refused this latest offer and no other offer was on the table. The lawyer's view was that she thought she could not improve on the offer and it was likely that a tribunal would make a lesser award if indeed they decided she had been unfairly dismissed. It was clear the union would not represent her and we left. As we walked along West George Street into the town, I asked her if what she was offered would cover her teacher training. She indicated it would and I thought some more as we walked. We stopped at the junction with Hope Street.

'Take the money,' I said, 'become a teacher - it's an honourable profession.'

She took this advice in the same way she had taken the other advice I'd given her and has been teaching ever since. I have never really met anyone who trusted me so much and I was relieved when she called me later to say she had sent a letter accepting the offer.

It was not too long before I was back in the same mode with another colleague. His case was surprisingly similar, in that proper procedures were being ignored when dealing with his absence management. Moreover, his manager was inclined to make somewhat inane remarks at meetings. I advised him to record their next meeting surreptitiously which he did and it produced some damaging statements from the management. In particular, when my colleague mentioned his discussion of his position with a lawyer. The manager questioned how he could pay a lawyer when he was off sick and remarked, 'It must be one of those cheap lawyers.'

It was an idiotic thing to say, but that is how idiots react and it later cost the firm a considerable sum. I then wrote a number of letters on my friend's behalf and finally they were forced into dismissing him.

I remember I was in my garden when I got a call from a director making an offer to avoid a tribunal. I refused to accept it and reminded him we had a tape that I would seek to have admitted as evidence of bullying tactics at the tribunal. I gave him a minimum figure I would accept and he refused to consider it. He went on to say that, as his manager was not aware she was being taped, the tape would be inadmissible. I told him it was not his or my decision as to what was or was not admissible at an Employment Tribunal. It was up to the chairman to decide what evidence he would hear or not hear. I then advised him that the chairman was bound to try and resolve the case fairly. It was the chairman and only the chairman who decided admissibility, and I was prepared to take my chances with the tape. I also said that regardless of what happened with the tape he ought to listen to it and see what kind of manager this particular person was. He had, of course, already done so. He finally said he would consider what I'd said and call back. Two hours later he called and offered what I had asked for. I told him I knew it would be acceptable and he should send the paper work and an agreement would be forthcoming. In the end they paid up and my friend resigned.

The management had adopted a policy of relaxing certain requirements such as the dress code on Fridays. 'Dress Down Day,' happened every Friday and staff were permitted to wear jeans, trainers, T-shirts and so on. Games of email bingo were played and jokes sent to everyone by email. The director, who had closed down my computer the day I was suspended over a year before, was now in some trouble due to an email he sent to staff. He had emailed what he thought was a joke on the Friday afternoon. It was unfunny and quite disgusting. Two female members of my team approached me at my desk almost immediately after it appeared and there was a buzz around the office. I told my staff I agreed with their view that the email was unacceptable but I was too busy to deal with it at the time. I promised I would do so first thing on Monday morning. I sensed that most female staff, and some of the men, were offended by what had been written.

On Monday morning I drafted a complaint against the director and sent it to my line manager. She was out of the office but called me later to say she had spoken with the director who was in London until the following Friday morning. She advised that he was preparing an apology that would be sent to all staff and took it that this would be an end of the matter. I disagreed and reminded her that if any other employee had sent a similar email, they would be facing disciplinary action. I also remarked that I did not see any reason why the director should be immune from such proceedings. I went on to say that I would raise a grievance through our contractual procedures as she was obviously uninterested in taking the matter seriously. She was not happy with my response but had to accept I had the right to do as I had said. She parted by saying she would speak further with the director. Before I left that evening, she called me to say she had again spoken with the director, and he would meet with me when he returned at the end of the week from London. I received an email from him that day advising that the meeting would be in his office at ten the following Friday.

I met with him in his office as arranged. Following the usual pleasantries, he gave me the floor and I asked what had possessed a man in his senior position to send out such an email. He really had no clear response, said he was sorry, and had reported the matter to his own superior. She would take whatever action she felt necessary and had already indicated it was a stupid thing to do. He was very apologetic and genuinely regretful and I accepted that he had simply made a really stupid mistake. He said as a manager, I was right to raise the issue and he bore no grudges. I told him that in light of what he'd said I would withdraw my grievance immediately.

He then went on to chat about work and told me he was aware I was opposed to many of the changes but they were necessary for the good of the business. He assured me that my job, and those of my team, were safe but we would have to consider making changes that fell within the new aims of the organisation. He finished by saying that his door was always open if I wanted to talk about anything. It was an ending that I remembered as the old year drew to a close.

Just before the Christmas holidays I emailed him and asked for a meeting in the New Year. He responded with a date and time and after the holidays we met in his office. I had the whole holiday period to think about my approach and was well prepared when we met in the middle of January. He began by asking me what I wanted to discuss.

'Redundancy,' I said. 'I want you to make me redundant.'

His response surprised me somewhat as he did not dismiss the idea out of hand but said that the company only followed the statutory requirements and I would not receive that much in terms of payment. I told him I had calculated what it would amount to with lying time and holiday payments due and it was a great deal more than I would receive when I was compulsory retired in two years' time. I passed him some figures and he said he would have a look at them. He also advised that even if the figures added up, he could not simply make someone redundant. In reality it was a job that was redundant not an individual person. The research team would still be there and would need a manager. I responded by saying they did not need a manager, that these individuals were more than capable of managing themselves and a team leader would suffice to carry out appraisals, manage absences and discipline. The team could do the rest themselves. Team leaders were paid considerably less than I was, I reminded him, and the two years and some months I had left would more than recover the redundancy payments if I was gone. In fact, it would be a considerable saving. I had said all I could and it was now up to him. He said he would discuss it further with the Board and I should perhaps re-consider my position but I was adamant I wanted to leave.

I had an anxious few days waiting for his call until it finally arrived.

'Can you come into my office for a few minutes John?'

I put my phone down and hurried along, knocked on the door and entered. I tried to gauge his mood but he was quite poker faced. He had my notes from our last meeting in front of him on his desk and it was clear that my redundancy request was what the meeting was about.

'I have to tell you I have spoken with the Board and recommended they accept your proposal. They have done so and you will receive the paperwork in a day or so. We will also pay up to fifty pounds for you to have the agreement checked over by a lawyer.'

'So that's it, John. Personally, I know your job is not in jeopardy but I accept the retirement issues and wish you a happy retirement. Unless of course you are looking for another job.'

'I've been working since I left school at the age of fifteen - that's almost forty-seven years, including my time at college and university. I think that's plenty. Meanwhile I thank you for your support with this. I know it has not been easy.'

With that I left his office and went back to my desk quite elated. A few days later the promised paperwork arrived from London. It looked fine to me but I took it to a lawyer across

189

from the office and he read it through while I sat in his office. He opined that it was a standard agreement but he expressed a little doubt about a particular clause. It prevented me from setting up a similar business within a few miles of the office and he asked me if this could present a problem sometime in the future.

'You've seen the amount of redundancy payment,' I said. 'I really don't think that comes close to what it would cost to set up a similar business. In any case, I am sick of working in a call centre. The clause is fine so I'll sign it in your presence and trouble you no further.'

We shook hands and that was that. My wife was impressed by the speed by which my employers responded to my request for redundancy.

'They really must have wanted rid of you,' she said.

No specific date was set for my leaving and it was left to me to go when I saw fit. I did not want to leave my team or my successor in the dark about my work with Contributor Access or other parts of the BBC, so I wrote a report on my activities with a list of BBC contacts. When I finished my report, I passed it to my line manager and we had a short meeting about its contents. I told her then I did not want any of the usual leaving festivities and would go in a couple of days after I contacted some colleagues in BBC London. I then had a meeting with my team and I told them I was going. There was a variety of responses but they were in agreement that it was the best thing for me in the circumstances. I told them they were welcome to a small party in the Pot Still once I arranged it with the owner, Kenny. I made a few calls, sent a few emails and left the office for the last time early that afternoon. I went into the Pot Still. I was a free man for the first time in eleven years.

It had been a wonderful experience being a part of the BBC for all those years. It had been a long steady climb up a learning curve and when I checked back our records, we had covered over three-thousand different topics since Helpline opened. I had met people from many cultural backgrounds and walks of life, but for the most part they all had the same love of the BBC and were passionate in their desire to help people with real problems. They were a delightful bunch to work with and really knew how to throw a party. At one of our nights out I won a food voucher for singing but I knew it was a sympathy vote when my guitarist accompanist got pissed and turned up half way through the song playing an out-of-tune guitar. We had some great evenings supporting *Children in Need* and I remember our director of that time sitting in a pub on Sauchiehall Street in a full Pudsey Bear outfit, including the head. Two good-looking girls walked past him and he invited them to our party in the Central Hotel.

'Just ask for me,' he said and the girls ran off laughing.

'Do you know what you just did?' I asked, 'you've just told those girls to turn up at the Central Hotel and tell the doorman Pudsey Bear sent them.'

At another CIN party my friend Ray and I were set to sing a duet to raise money for the charity. We chose *Matchstalk Men and Matchstalk Cats and Dogs* and billed ourselves in emails as the 'Sweat Shop Boys.' Unfortunately, this upset the management, who at the time were trying to deal with press enquiries about alleged bullying at the Helpline. One last CIN memory involved me getting a makeover with mascara, face powder, lipstick and a ribbon in my hair. The girls offered to do this for a £2 donation but despite their pressure I refused. Eventually I agreed to have it done if they raised fifty pounds from other staff before the end of my shift. Less than twenty minutes later they were at my desk with the money. 'You're on,' they said and I had no option. I smoked in those days but you had to go outside. I went downstairs on to Sauchiehall Street and was joined by a colleague who was wearing a pair of white ladies' knickers over his trousers and holding a flowery pink cup and saucer in one hand and smoking a fag through a long cigarette holder with the other. Suddenly I looked across the street and half-a-dozen Russian sailors were staring over at us. I looked at my colleague and told him that, big as he was, if he waved or made any gestures at all I'd kick him in a sensitive area. Of course, he waved over and they immediately marched off. I expect when they got back to Moscow, they had plenty to say about Glasgow, that decadent capitalist city.

Of course, there were some difficult times at the end but the culture had changed by then. Overall, it was the best job I have ever had. Most of the subjects we researched were serious matters, but we also had many laughs. Every Christmas we got a call from someone, usually a primary school teacher, asking for the names of Santa's reindeer. I developed the habit of sending an email around with the detail of the nine names. In the email I advised that a colleague may try to convince them there was a tenth reindeer called Olive but to ignore him. I was at my desk when one of the telephone agents called me over and said she had a caller on the line asking for the reindeer names. I saw she was about to use my email to answer it and made my way back to my desk. When I sat down, I heard her tell the caller that some people say there was another reindeer called Olive, as in 'Olive the other reindeer.' Even when I tried to explain it was a joke as in: 'All of the other reindeer …' she still didn't get it. I could hardly get on with my work for laughing. A colleague swears he heard one of the BBC agents say to a caller: 'The postcode is 7TQ, T for Tommy, Q for cucumber.'

During my time with the BBC and in previous employments I had met and spoken with some well-known celebrities. Away from the BBC I'd had Scottish comedian Lex MacLean, a regular customer in the off-licence on West Nile Street that I managed, along with Rikki Fulton and Jack Milroy, or Francie and Jose, as they were better known. Andy

Stewart's agent Max was also a customer but I never met Andy who, despite his public image, was a non-drinker.

One of my most memorable meetings was with the famous American star, Eartha Kitt. I met her by accident at a coffee bar in Renfield Street opposite the Classic Cinema owned by the former Ranger's player, George Young. Myself and my workmate, John Boyle, who was Rangers daft, went there for lunch a few times a week and chatted with some of the well-known Rangers players of the time including Jim Baxter, Davy Wilson and Ian MacMillan. On that particular morning we were talking with Davy Wilson and Jim Baxter about the previous Saturday's match and left ourselves late for work. We ran downstairs and I bumped into a woman wearing a fancy fur coat and knocked her down. When I helped her to her feet, she was clearly annoyed. It was Eartha Kitt and she stormed off like a diva, disgusted to have come into contact with a working-class person. She was appearing at the Glasgow Empire at the time.

Another famous Rangers' player of those days was part-timer Ian MacMillan, who worked as an architect a few doors up from my place of work in West Regent Street. I saw him every day dressed in his suit and coat and looking nothing like the great player he was.

I also met Jet Harris, who was part of Cliff Richard's backing group, The Shadows. I met him in McCall's Bar on Hope Street, now the Pot Still, one afternoon when I had a day off from work. I was in the darts room on my own when I noticed a guy at the bar asking, in a cockney accent, for a large blue vodka. He looked very much out-of-step with what the normal Glasgow boy was wearing at the time. He had dyed-blonde hair and wore a pale blue jacket, grey slacks and black Italian winklepicker shoes. He came into the darts room and asked if I wanted to play, so we played a few games and got talking about Cliff Richard and the Shadows. He was in Glasgow because his girlfriend was appearing in a children's version of *Juke Box Jury* on Scottish Television later that afternoon. He invited me to accompany him to the STV studio in Hope Street but before I agreed I asked if he could do me a favour. I told him I used to work in an office across the road and asked if he would come with me to meet my mate, John, who still worked there. The firm employed a large number of payroll clerks, all female, and I really wanted them to see me with this famous guy. He was up for it, and for weeks later I became known as the guy who knew Cliff Richard and the Shadows. I often wonder who put the story around the Locarno dance hall.

When I was about ten years old, I was with a group of other kids around that age in the lane behind the Empire Theatre in Glasgow. The American country singer Slim Whitman was top of the bill. We were shouting his name when suddenly he appeared at an open window, sat on the ledge and sang a few bars of *China Doll*. It was a wonderful moment and we could not wait to tell our parents when we got home.

I also had a chat with golfer Gary Player, many years later in Birmingham's New Street Railway station. He had just finished a tournament at Turnberry, but there was a strike at Glasgow Airport and he could not get his flight to take part in the Spanish Open. Alternative arrangements were made and he was flying out from Birmingham Airport on a private jet. I was picking up a new truck and delivering it to London. We spoke as we walked along the platform and I told him I thought he had a beautiful home. He asked me if I'd been to South Africa, and I had to tell him I'd only seen it on a television documentary.

However, despite meeting some well-known celebrities over the years, the most memorable was not a human being. I was delivering a load of gas meters that I'd picked up in London for the Southport Gas Board. After I unloaded, I drove to a car park next to the beach to make some tea on my primus stove. The rain was lashing down and the car park was deserted, save for one, very wet, carpark attendant. I invited him into the lorry out of the rain and offered him a cup of tea.

'This tastes very nice,' he said, as he sipped at the warm beverage.

'That's because it's made with Scottish water,' I told him. I explained I carried a couple of gallons of Scottish tap water on each trip as tea made with English water tasted awful. 'Full of chalk,' I said. Our conversation turned to racehorses and the fact that the three-time Grand National winner and twice runner-up, Red Rum, trained along the Southport sands. He told me the stable was only a few miles along the road in Birkdale and if I had the time I should go and have a look. I asked for directions and he wrote them down on the back of my driver's log book. The rain subsided and I drove off in the direction of Birkdale. A few miles on I turned left and the scene was instantly recognisable from the television news pictures shown after each of his National wins. There, in front of me, was the railway level crossing and the car showroom. I parked the lorry and walked to the showroom. It was a wide pavement that held a couple of cars for sale and I looked inside. The walls were virtually covered with framed photos of Red Rum, so I went inside to ask if I could have look. A man was seated at a desk, who very much resembled the horse's trainer Ginger McCain, said there was no problem, so I walked around the small office, admiring the images. Outside I saw a horsebox draw up and a youngish man entered the office. The man behind the desk called me over and said: 'Billy here will take you round to the stable where you can see the real thing.' I was absolutely flabbergasted. He told me the horsebox was taking Red Rum to the Sedgefield Races where he was opening some sort of fete. I was quite speechless as Billy led me around the side of the showroom to the stable. I don't know what I expected but it was not what I saw. It was an old stable with a squeaky gate, holes in the wood and hinges that were crooked and squealed when Billy drew the stable door open. Inside, enjoying some hay stood the most famous racehorse in the world. For some reason I expected him to be lodged in some palatial mansion like a Hollywood film star, but there he stood in an old stable with squeaky hinges. I went inside and patted him, feeling like I was in the presence of a very special being. I mentioned to Billy that the stable wasn't what I expected and he simply said. 'He's a horse, where would you expect him to live?' I mentioned that I'd read that a Japanese consortium wanted to buy the horse and asked if that was true. 'Rummy will never leave Southport,' he said, 'the people of this town would burn us at the stake if we sold him to anyone.'

My journey home was very pleasant indeed with a memory I would surely never forget. I was with Janet at a party one night and someone asked me what was the best thing that had ever happened to me. I had no hesitation. 'Meeting Red Rum,' I said. 'What about our wedding day?' Janet asked, so Red Rum was demoted to second best. This was a time long before mobile phones and selfies, which is a shame. I would love to have had a photo of me with the most famous racehorse in the world.

I have met many famous people but my worst memory is about one I did not get to meet. I was in London for a few meetings spread over four days ending with a visit to the Jimmy Young programme on the Friday morning. On the Thursday evening I was in my hotel room around six when I got a call from a female colleague. She told me she had arrived earlier in the day and had visited the Radio 2 studio that afternoon. We arranged to meet for a meal later that night. We were sitting in a small Italian restaurant near the BBC Portland Place studios when she said she had something to tell me and I would likely kill her when she did. I suggested that killing her was highly unlikely, as whatever it was it could not be that bad. How wrong I was. Whilst waiting in the Green Room for the programme to finish, in walked one of the biggest stars in the world: Tony Bennett. All it would have taken was a phone call, and I would have stopped whatever I was doing, and somehow got to the studio. I would have been able to walk in there, meet my idol, and have a wee chat with him. One lousy call would have done it. She was right enough, I felt like killing her and I'm sure if I'd come before a judge who liked music I'd have walked on a plea of temporary insanity.

Chapter Fifteen

Have Bus Pass Will Travel

On my first day of retirement nobody phoned, nobody emailed, nobody asked a question and nobody had a complaint to resolve. Of course, it was like this on holidays, but this was different. Consigned to obscurity, I adopted a 'have bus-pass will travel' outlook and if I could get there and back in a day, I went. I visited museums, art galleries and racecourses around the country. I have always liked horses from my early years with my grandfather and first went horse-racing in my teens and spent a lot of time trying to beat the bookie. But as the saying goes: 'You can't beat a bookie with a big stick.' I spend a lot of my time in bookies and they have been a non-exhaustive source of problems to resolve. In my first year of retirement I dealt with a few consumer complaints and a criminal injury compensation claim, when two men forced their way into a man's house and beat him up in their search for money. I represented people at tribunals and, following my name appearing in a *Sunday Mail* article, received requests for assistance from a few other claimants. The issues were varied, and the one appeal I lost was in an Industrial Disablement benefit claim where the claimant was held not to be deaf enough, despite the fact he had worked in the noisy engineering environment for over thirty years and was prescribed two hearing aids. These cases kept me from becoming too bored but in any event, I always had my writing to fall back on.

I had been writing poetry for many years and at the beginning I tried to have some of it published, which is the literary equivalence of King Canute trying to hold back the sea. Those publishers who bothered to write back generally said it didn't meet with their genre, or it was too political for their readers.

I also tried my hand at writing radio drama, which I first listened to on the Home Service when I was a young boy. After I had completed two plays, I sent them to the BBC. This was back in 1988 but I still have the rejection letter. On one play the criticism was that it was rather formulaic and did nothing to differentiate it from other police dramas, which I disagreed with, as one would expect from a writer. On the other hand, they were more encouraging about the second play, writing: '...the drama manages to move beyond formula into something more genuinely felt about the politics of modern policing, and the events and characters have a reality that is lacking in the other play.' They did invite me to submit other work but it was many years before I did so, and the response had changed little. Now the BBC have a system for submissions that is so technical I wonder why anyone bothers. For a start you can only submit one piece of work at a time and only during specified windows.

I have written a number of dramas since those days including a play about Russian revolutionary, Sergey Nechayev, that an internet radio broadcaster agreed to publish but, after months of waiting for something to happen, I told them to forget it and destroy their copy of my manuscript.

I've written a black comedy about Mrs Thatcher, who gets dumped outside an old folk's home on the Yorkshire Moors, and another about a woman who blames the local council for her husband's suicide and exacts a terrible revenge on Guy Fawkes' Night. I've also had a go at writing short stories including one entitled *Thirteen Seconds*, which was the average time it took the most famous hangman of all time, Albert Pierrepoint, to despatch convicted murderers. Pierrepoint held the job from 1934 until the abolition of capital punishment in 1965. He executed over 450 people in his lifetime, including Nazi war criminals, and was a feared man among kids in Glasgow who were told if they didn't behave Albert would get them. It is said that Pierrepoint could remove the condemned from their cell, stand them on the trap, bind their hands behind their back, place a blindfold over their eyes and pull the lever in just over twelve seconds.

The one thing I had not written was a full-length novel but just before I retired, I was working on a novel entitled *Golden Eyes*. This was a sequel to one of my favourite novels, *The Midwich Cuckoos* by John Wyndham, and was based fifty years after the original. The title was a reference to the golden-eyed children in Wyndham's novel and many of the characters and settings in my book came from Wyndham's pen. Consequently, before I sent it to a publisher, I had to clear some copyright issues and set about trying to contact Wyndham's estate. Eventually I was in touch with the John Wyndham Archive at the University of Liverpool Library, who pointed me in the way of an address in Tasmania. I wrote, explaining my novel and asked if someone would respond but no one ever did. That is something a writer just has to accept. After all, you are approaching total strangers either trying to sell them a book, a play or a poem or trying to get information from them. You are in the junk mail business whether you accept it or not. I still have the manuscript for the Wyndham sequel and, every now and then, I consider sending it to a publisher but I have not done so yet. Perhaps I'm not as immune to rejection slips as I once was.

The trouble with retirement is keeping occupied and avoiding the temptation to become a couch tottie. If the latter is the strength of your ambition you may as well invite the grim reaper for lunch. The free bus-pass is a wonderful thing and in my early retirement years I would go to Buchanan Street Bus Station and get on the next bus going somewhere I had not been in a while. I also love boats, and living on the west coast, I'm never far away from a ferry: Ardrossan to Arran, Largs to Millport, Wemyss Bay to Rothesay, Gourock to Dunoon or Kilcreggan, and there's the *Waverley* paddle steamer when its boiler isn't being repaired or it isn't crashing into a pier.

My favourite day out, weather permitting, is to take a bus to Gourock and the ferry over to Kilcreggan. I get another bus to the Gareloch where I stop for lunch, then on to Helensburgh, and then a train back into Glasgow in time for a beer in the Pot Still. It sounds a busy day but it's only around six or seven hours, or a bit more if you like taking photographs which I do. Anyway, what else have you got to do if you're retired?

I was sitting on Kilcreggan Pier one lovely afternoon looking across the bay to Gourock and enjoying the peace when suddenly I remembered that just over the hill at my back sat a major Russian missile target. Life sometimes shatters you back to reality when you don't want to be there. Sitting there I thought about the thousands of ships that passed through these waters over the centuries on their way across the Atlantic or bound for Australia. I remembered old Donald McKinnon, who was a student of mine during my days with adult education. Donald was in the Royal Navy during the war and sailed from Greenock to join the Russian arctic convoys in 1945 on his ship the *Lapwing*. It was torpedoed near Murmansk, and Donald was one of sixty-one survivors. Fifteen sailors were lost.

When I had him as a student, he was invited to the Russian Embassy in Glasgow to receive a medal for his war contribution. He brought it to our next meeting at my request. I noted that the small booklet he was given with the medal was written in Russian. I asked him if he knew what it said but he didn't. I went on to ask why he hadn't asked one of the people at the Embassy to translate it for him but he said he didn't like to ask. He'd been torpedoed, his lungs were filled with oil, his hands were frozen to the ropes on a raft and he thought he was going to die, but he didn't like to ask. What a guy!

When the QE2 was being built at John Brown's shipyard I worked in the nearby Clydebank Bar. The ship returned to Greenock in 2007 and I went to see it. The rain lashed down and I was soaked through and none too pleased when I saw the powers that be had berthed her next to a load of containers that blocked most of the view of her sleek lines. It was a public relations disaster as far as I was concerned, and the best I could make of it was to video the shambles and upload it to YouTube.

The previous year the MV *Kenilworth* passenger ferry from Kilcreggan to Gourock was caught up in a NATO warship exercise. A United States frigate sent a radio message saying it would fire on unidentified ships as the Kenilworth crossed the warship's path. A Naval Base spokesman said it was a 'regrettable incident' but stressed the ferry was in no danger. I wrote the following at the time sung to the tune of *The Tangle o'the Isles*.

I waas sailing from Kilcregan o'er to Gourock 'cross the bay
The journey had an element of farce
For the Captain of a frigate telt me tae go away
Or he'd blow a big torpedo up ma arse
Now the sail aboard the Kenilworth is often chust sublime
And oor Captain Para Handy doesn't flinch
So he telt the US Navy tae go and get a life
And he wiznae gonni move a fuckin' inch
But the Captain of the frigate wouldn't warrant such discourse
So he ordered all his weapons to be primed
Then he signalled Para Handy that he should alter course
Or he'd blow him oot the waater, he wiz warned
Para Handy didnae worry but set sail for Tobermory where he knew the pubs stayed opened past their 'oors

Then he telt the US Skipper he wiz nothin' but a kipper
And his navy run by fifty dollar whores
The signal wisnae clever and upset the US skipper of the
frigate That he thought waas chust sublime
So he launched his big torpedo and his other bombs beside
And soon the world waas running out of time
Now you may think its facile tae argue wi a missile on the
firth Of Clyde or any other place
That's why Captain Para Handy and McPhail the engineer
and the cabin boy are sunk without a trace
Now this story is quite gory they never got tae Tobermory
where the pubs stay open long beyond their time
But they're sittn'up in hivvin, sippin whiskies by the dizen
And thinking that their life is chust sublime.

Cranstonhill Swimming Baths

Chapter Sixteen

The Loss of my son, James

The 19th of December 2007 through to the early hours of the next day was, and will remain, the worst hours of my life. It started with a call from Coatbridge Hospital to say that James had been admitted and was very unwell. I arranged to borrow a van from a family friend, Martha, and set off to see him. When I arrived, I was told he had been transferred to Hairmyres Hospital in East Kilbride. I got there around 1pm to be met by a grim-faced surgeon who told me James was seriously ill with heart disease. He had contacted heart consultants at Glasgow's Western Infirmary who opined that if they operated, he would 'die on the table.' The surgeon's conclusion at this time was that James was: 'in the hands of God.' If by some miracle he came through, the surgeon told me, he would be confined to a wheelchair and would need a transplant.

I went in to see him and joked that he was trying to outdo his mum, who'd survived a heart attack.

'It's worse than that, Dad.' he said.

I sat speaking with him for a while but he was falling in and out of consciousness and being monitored by nurses and doctors. I called Janet and did the best I could to tell her what was going on and she was brought to the hospital by a family friend, Ian Cadwell. It was very emotional and some of James' friends had arrived, concerned about his condition. The hours went by with no improvement and when I went in to see him, he was complaining of being very thirsty, but I was told I could only wet his lips with an ice cube. He was clearly very tired and I suggested that the visitors would be better going home to get some rest. I told Janet I thought she would be better off at home and I would call her immediately if there was any news. When everyone was gone, I lay on the bed in the small room I had been given to stay as long as necessary. Memories of his childhood ran through my head as I lay staring up at the ceiling.

James was a big boy when he was born and was over six feet in his early teens. He was quite an awkward kid and was always bumping into things, tripping on stairs and falling off his bike. On one occasion, when we stayed in Glasgow, he was bent over with severe stomach pain and we took him to the Sick Children's Hospital at Kelvinhaugh. Janet and I noticed that the examining doctor was looking suspiciously at some bruises on his leg. We advised the doctor that James collected bruises like other children collected football cards and he was happy to accept he was not an abused child. In the event, he was stricken by severe constipation and was kept in overnight. I collected him in my lorry the following morning and he was as right as rain.

James did very well at school, primary and secondary. In his senior years he achieved very high marks in O-Grades and Highers and won an award for the best 'Modern Studies' essay when he was fourteen. He was a member of the school chess team at Greenwood Academy and travelled round the country playing for the team. They were a formidable group, winning many prizes in competitions against other schools and James never forgot to send postcards from wherever he was. I had taught him the basic moves of chess when he was about ten, but by the time he was fourteen, I could not come close to beating him. In 1990 I entered the 'Tournament of the Mind' test run by Mensa and the *The Times*. The questions were in the paper each day for a couple of weeks but I struggled with the mathematics and science questions, so I enlisted his help. He found most of the questions very easy, whilst I hardly understood the question let alone the answer. In the end I got a certificate saying I had achieved over ninety percent but it was James who should have got it, not me. When he was fourteen, we won an under-fifteen father and son snooker competition at our local hall. Because James was almost six feet tall at the time, I had to convince the sceptical committee that he was only fourteen before they would hand over our medals and the cup. Although I did question why they had not sought to confirm his age at the start of the tournament, rather than the end. I still have the cup at home as the club went bankrupt within the next year.

James stayed on at school until he was seventeen when he was accepted for a place at Glasgow University to study engineering. He stayed for a while with my mother in Glasgow but it was not a very satisfactory arrangement. She was a difficult woman to get on with no matter what kind of nature you had and I did not think he was very happy there and suggested he came home for weekends. On one weekend home he asked me to go for a pint at my local as he had something he wanted to talk about. When we got talking in the pub, he asked me how I would feel if he gave up his university course. I said that university education was not for everyone and the majority of people managed well enough without it, I added that if he was leaving university because he had other plans then his mum and I would help all we could but if he intended to lie on the couch and watch television, he would get plenty of grief from me. It was then he told me he had got a position at Volunteer Services Overseas in London for a couple of years and was leaving the next day. I walked him to the bus stop on the Sunday evening - he was very quiet and I thought a bit apprehensive.

'You don't have to do this,' I said. 'You can go back to the house, unpack and consider what other options you have tomorrow, but remember this: if you want to come home at any point, I will be there to pick you up in less than ten hours. Your dad's an old trucker, remember.'

The bus arrived and he got on-board, and it was my turn to feel a bit sad and apprehensive. When he got there, he went to work with a young paraplegic boy who had injured himself in a swimming pool accident. He spent two years with the boy before beginning training as a student psychiatric nurse at Brentwood Hospital. Whilst there he met and became great friends with Sanjeev, a student from Mauritius. On his first Christmas as a student he and Sanjeev travelled to Scotland to stay with us over the holiday. Sanjeev was a lovely young man, quite small, very well dressed with shirt, collar and tie, three-piece suit, highly polished shoes and short back and sides haircut. James, on the other hand, looked like he'd glued himself when naked and then run through a charity shop; he also sported Rastafarian dreadlocks.

They hired a car, and I drove them along the banks of Loch Lomond and north to Inverary. Sanjeev kept saying he hadn't seen a Scotsman wearing a kilt but I was confident that, in the lay-by on the Rest and be thankful, a guy in full highland dress would be playing the bagpipes next to the hotdog stall. When we reached the lay-by, the stall was closed and there was no piper. We had some lunch in Inverary and after spending some time looking around the town we started back. We got into Glasgow around seven o'clock and still hadn't seen a man in a kilt. We went into a pub on St. Enoch Square and after a few minutes a guy appeared in full highland dress handing round leaflets for the SNP. He made Sanjeev very happy and I thought he was going to join the Scottish National Party at one point.

With the holiday over, the student nurses set off for London on an overnight train from Glasgow. James phoned home soon after they arrived at Euston and told me that when he and Sanjeev were walking through Euston Station in the early hours of the morning, they were stopped by two policemen. The police asked them what they were doing and James said they were a couple of drug dealers, explaining quickly they were student nurses at Brentwood, and had just returned for a holiday in Scotland. Having satisfied the police about their credentials both parties wished each other a happy new year and were set to go their separate ways when one policeman asked if he could ask one more question. 'I don't mean to be racist,' he said, 'but haven't you two guys got your haircuts mixed up?'

James remained a student for a while but later left to become a chef. When I pointed out that he had qualifications that were not exactly those required of a chef he pointed out that all cookery is just chemistry. He then came home and went back to university to study for a degree in hotel management. On completion of his degree he was employed as a chef in hotels and restaurants across the country. He won competitions, chiefly for desserts, and on his visits home we enjoyed meals that were far removed from our normal diets. He worked at the Broadford Hotel on Skye and the family enjoyed a number of visits to see him. On one visit James paid for a hire car and I drove him and his younger brother, Stephen, around the island. We finished our tour in Portree, where the locals were enjoying an open-air ceilidh and it was a very memorable day.

At this time James had a girlfriend, Amanda, who also worked in the hotel industry and they started talking about going to Australia. Their idea was to spend a year there and work their way around the country. They saved until they had enough money put together to satisfy the Australian authorities that they were self-sufficient and set off. Over the next year they travelled around the country picking up work here and there, eating lemon ants in the bush and sweltering under the heat at Ayres Rock. We received regular postcards, photographs and letters enabling the family to follow their trails and it seemed like they were having the time of their lives. I have not got round turning these into a book celebrating my son's life but in some way it is still too soon. Despite his mum's worries about him being so far away, he returned home safe and sound with loads of presents for the family, including the inevitable boomerangs and Maori paintings.

He returned to his beloved Glasgow and obtained work chiefly in Italian restaurants and at the time he was taken to hospital he was with Fratellis working between their restaurants in Cambuslang and Coatbridge. It was from his flat in Coatbridge he was taken to hospital. As I lay there with these thoughts running through my head, a nurse entered the room. It was around three o'clock in the morning.

'I think it's time, Mr Keeman,' she said.

I followed her into the ward and James was lying on his bed asleep. He looked very poorly and within a few minutes he was gone. I held his hand for a while, kissed him and left crying my eyes out. I walked around outside, lost, alone and afraid to call Janet to tell her the news. It took a while before I could face phoning, but eventually I did. It was the hardest thing I'd ever had to do as a father and I'm sure all those people who have had to tell a mother that her son is dead know how it feels. Life sometimes gives you the courage needed to get through the bad times, and I was grateful for it then. I went back into the hospital and spoke with the surgeon about possible transplant options. I knew James would be willing to be a donor but his major organs were too badly damaged to be of use. However, the surgeon explained to me that ligaments and tendons can be transplanted in children who have suffered accident damage and can enable them to play football again or ride a bike. I called Janet on the phone and asked what she thought. Like me she was sure James would approve so we agreed and a transplant co-ordinator came to talk me through the process. I signed the papers and was advised James would be moved to Gartnavel Hospital who had the facilities for dealing with transplant organs. I was absolutely outraged when the undertaker charged an extra £100 to move James from Hairmyres to Gartnavel.

Over the next few days we arranged the funeral and chose to have a humanist service. I called the Humanist Society and spoke with a former BBC colleague, Gordon Ross, who put me in touch with a local celebrant, as they're known. Gordon himself had many health problems, including Parkinson's Disease, and campaigned through the courts for the right to die. He was unsuccessful, but finally succumbed to his illnesses in 2016. I attended his funeral along with a friend. It too was a humanist celebration and some of the speeches and stories about Gordon's life and times were very funny and moving at the same time.

When Janet and I got out of the car at the crematorium, there was an enormous crowd of people waiting, the majority unknown to us. I introduced Janet as his mum and myself as his dad. Soon it was over and we now had to try and pick up the pieces. James' boss arranged for the Cambuslang restaurant to be reserved for the meal and I travelled to Glasgow with a friend of James and a young girl who James had trained as a chef. She was in a terrible state of grief and it was difficult to console her. I later met her mum who said James had been so helpful in supporting her daughter who was now doing very well as a hotel chef in the city. It was very surreal at the restaurant with one Italian after another approaching my table to offer their condolences and it was only then I realised how well liked and respected my son was by those in his chosen profession. A BBC colleague gave me a lift into Glasgow and I went for a pint in the Pot Still where I sat alone trying to picture what the future held for me, Janet and my other two sons.

All these years later we still think of James every day and I know we will do so until we have taken our last breath. Sometimes it is a small comfort to know that James will not have to face the aches and pains, illness, disease and loss of dignity that old age can bring but if I'm truthful, my selfishness makes me wish he was still here. He was a wonderful son for thirty-seven years and we are grateful and proud to have been his parents.

Some weeks after the funeral, a Turkish girl arrived at our door in a taxi. She asked Janet if James was at home and when Janet told her James was dead, she said it was young James she was looking for, not his dad. Janet did what she could to explain there was no old James and that his dad's name was John. When she understood she thrust a parcel into Janet's hand, saying it was a present for James and cried her way back to the taxi. I stopped the cab from driving away until I had the chance to speak with her, after which I returned the package. It was between her and James. She told me my son had worked with her father in the catering business and he'd been friends with her for a while. He'd told her when she came back over to Scotland, she should look him up, and she did, but to be met by this terrible news. We never heard from her again.

Shortly afterwards Sanjeev phoned. He had not seen James for a few years and was now a qualified psychologist at a Birmingham Hospital with a wife and young children. He had lost the last address he had for James and he also had to be given the awful news. He was shocked when I told him and I promised to send him a copy of a DVD I'd made as a celebration of his life. There were other incidences like this but eventually they faded as time went past.

I found in the months following his death that I could only get some respite through writing. James and I used to argue about boxing and who was the greatest heavyweight boxer ever. He admired Muhammad Ali but I favoured Rocky Marciano. I started to research a book on the history of heavyweight boxing champions from 1865 until 1965, which I dedicated to James when it was finished. Without my writing I do not know how I would have coped. I sat in one library or another almost every day and could only get relief from my pain by concentrating on reading and writing. But eventually the grief began to subside and I began to feel a bit more positive about things. There is a line from a song that says 'Every time you go away you take a piece of me with you.' That's what it's like when someone you love dies. A little piece of you dies with them. My first thought when I wake up in the morning is of James. A big piece of me died when he did.

James and Sanjeev

Chapter Seventeen

A Cardiac Event

In March 2008 I visited my doctor with a chest complaint. I had been diagnosed with emphysema and asthma due to my many years as a heavy smoker and although I had given up two years before I was quite prone to infections. He asked me if anyone had spoken to me about a blood test result from two weeks previous and I told him they had not. He advised that the test revealed the presence of an enzyme that was only ever present if there was a heart problem and asked me to wait outside while he called the hospital to confirm the test result. A few minutes later he called me into his office, said he had confirmed the result with the hospital and that the hospital wanted to carry out some tests. Thinking it would be some way off I asked if he had any idea when I would be admitted.

'Today,' he said, 'and if you are driving, I would suggest you don't. Get someone to take you to Crosshouse Hospital as soon as you can. I'll give you a letter to take with you.'

The irony was that I had dropped Stephen at the hospital earlier and he was waiting for me to pick him up. When I arrived late, driven by a friend, it was as an in-patient.

I was seen by an Australian doctor who poked and prodded and hooked me up to a variety of monitors. Eventually he concluded that I'd had a 'cardiac event,' which I took as a euphemism for a heart attack. He asked if I'd had any severe chest pain or felt really sick recently and I recalled that two weeks before, on a Sunday afternoon, I had felt quite ill and went to bed. Janet was on holiday, but John and Stephen were at home. I told Stephen I had a sore chest and didn't feel well and was going for a lie down. I assumed it was another chest infection firing up and took a glass of hot orange and a couple of aspirin and crawled into bed. I told the Australian doctor that when I awoke some hours later and went downstairs, I was quite tired and lacking in energy and these feelings lasted until the following Tuesday when I felt more or less back to normal. Although I felt okay, I kept the appointment with my GP and it was during this appointment when the blood test that brought me to the hospital was taken.

'You did not have a chest infection,' the hospital doctor said. 'The blood tests and monitors confirm you had a cardiac event, but things seem to have settled. Nevertheless, we'll keep you here for a few days for observation and prescribe you some pills that may prevent a re-occurrence.'

Six days later I was discharged with the knowledge that I would hear from Ayr County Hospital about attending for an angiogram. Some weeks later I got my appointment through and went along quite apprehensive. The test concluded that I needed a heart-bypass operation and would be called for an appointment at the Jubilee Hospital in Clydebank. When this appointment came, I drove to the hospital not knowing what to expect.

The heart surgeon I saw advised me he did not think an operation at that time would improve my condition much and felt the tablets would suffice. He asked me for my view and I said I did not think it made sense to go through an operation of this nature if it was not going to achieve much. In the end we agreed to leave things as they were and I would be monitored as an out-patient and put on medication. This monitoring continued for almost two years, until a surgeon decided it could be stopped, but I was to continue with the medication for the rest of my life. During that time, I often wondered why I survived and James did not.

I had continued with my writing and during my research

into heavyweight boxing champions, I came across a story I could scarcely believe. It was a short piece in an old boxing magazine that said the American, Jack Johnson, the first black heavyweight champion of the world, had been initiated into the Freemasons in Dundee in October 1911. I trawled the internet but there was little clarification of the story so I re-read a biography of the boxer published in 2004: *Unforgivable Blackness: The Rise and Fall of Jack Johnson*. Nowhere in the book did I find a reference to the freemason story and I turned to Dundee University library for assistance. I emailed the library and asked if anyone had heard of Jack Johnson being initiated into the Freemasons in 1911. It was not long before I received a reply which delighted me. The library had copies of a few lengthy newspaper articles about the case published by the *Dundee Courier* and the *Edinburgh Gazette*. The email said that the articles covered the story up until the hearing by the Grand Lodge in Edinburgh which intrigued me even more and I couldn't wait to get copies of the articles.

A couple of days later they arrived by post and I spent an afternoon digesting this amazing story. In summary, Johnson was in Britain giving exhibitions of his boxing skills in theatres around the country. He was performing in Newcastle when he met Sydney McLaglen, the manager of a Music Hall artiste known as *Annie Abbot: The Little Georgia Magnet*. The two men got talking over a few drinks and McLaglen told Johnson that his artiste had been performing in Dundee during the previous week and he'd been invited to become a Freemason by some members of Lodge 225 in the city's Meadow Street. Johnson asked his companion what a Freemason was, and by the time McLaglen had finished his explanation Johnson was set on becoming a member himself. A telegram was sent to the Master of the Lodge, a Mister Blues, saying that the present heavyweight champion of the world wanted to become a member of the Lodge. A reply telegram invited Johnson to appear at the

Lodge the following Friday. The boxer, and his socialite wife, accompanied by McLaglen, set off from Newcastle the next day. On arriving in the early hours, they booked into the Royal Hotel. Prior to the champion's arrival word had spread within the freemason community and some members were opposed to the idea and expressing their disquiet. Those in favour of the initiation secretly changed the time of the meeting so that they could get the vote to go their way and the ceremony went ahead. Johnson later emerged from the meeting to be greeted by a large crowd who followed him all the way to the station and cheered until his train left for England.

When the news reached the United States, telegrams sailed across the Atlantic from the American Grand Lodge demanding Johnson's expulsion. Eventually and inevitably, Johnson's initiation was annulled by the Grand Lodge in Edinburgh and the decision was upheld on appeal. When he was given the news of the annulment Johnson told the reporter:

'I am a Freemason and as long as I live, I shall be one. Only God almighty can undo that...'

The story must be read in the context of the black man's position in the United States at that time. No black man would have been allowed to join a white lodge. Jim Crow laws meant blacks and whites were separated. Blacks could not eat in the same restaurants, attend the same schools, be buried in the same cemetery or travel in the same carriage on trains as a white man. A raft of other normal activities separated the races. The lynching of black people was a commonplace activity and the idea that a black man could become a Freemason was anathema to most white Americans.

Following my reading of Johnson and the Dundee Freemasons I penned an article and chose to send it to the *Scots Magazine*. In April 2009 I received a letter asking me to proof read the edited version for publication. At long last

I had convinced a publisher to publish a piece of my work. It was published in the following month's edition and was quite well received. This prompted another article, this time far removed from the boxing world but involving one of the most famous legal cases in the world that centred around the town of Paisley.

Prior to 1932 damages for negligence were based on a claimant having a contract with another party. There were occasions when a party with no contract could sue a manufacturer but only if the product in question was dangerous or fraudulently misrepresented. On a Sunday evening in August 1928, May Donoghue, a woman estranged from her husband and living with her parents in Glasgow's Gallowgate district, boarded a tram on Glasgow's High Street for her journey to Paisley. When she alighted at her stop she was met by her friend and they both walked the few hundred yards to the Wellmeadow Cafe. Her friend ordered and paid for a pear and ice cream for herself and an ice cream and ginger beer for May.

May later became ill with stomach pain, alleged to have been caused by the presence of a decomposing snail in her bottle of ginger beer. In an attempt to obtain compensation for her pain and suffering May contacted a lawyer but as she did not have a contract with the cafe owner, a case was brought against the manufacturer. All initial attempts to sue were dismissed by the Scottish courts, but the issue was appealed to the House of Lords. On the 20th of May 1932, Lord Atkin rose to deliver his speech which revealed his 'Neighbourhood Principle' to the rest of the world. Explaining his legal reasoning in a quiet, almost apologetic tone, he got to the crux of the decision:

'You must take care to avoid acts or omissions which you can reasonably foresee would be likely to injure your neighbour ...'

To his own question: 'Who then in law is my neighbour?' he answered: *'Persons who are so closely and directly affected by my act that I ought to have them in contemplation as being so affected when I am directing my mind to the acts or omissions which are called in question...'*

In simple terms David Stevenson should have been thinking of May Donohue when he was bottling his ginger beer.

In devastating form, Lord Atkin continued:

'...a manufacturer of products, which he sells in such a form as to show that he intends them to reach the ultimate consumer, in the form in which they left him with no reasonable possibility of intermediate examination, and with knowledge that the absence of reasonable care in the preparation or putting up of products will result in an injury to the consumer's life or property, owes a duty to the consumer to take reasonable care.'

That was it. A 'Duty of Care' was owed by a manufacturer to the ultimate consumer of his product and if on using the product an injury occurred the injured party could sue.

It opened the floodgates, particularly in the United States and gave rise to what we know at present as the 'No Win, No Fee' lawyer. People now sue for the slightest injury, physical or psychological. The case of *Donohue v Stevenson* opened the floodgates and billions of pounds have been handed over to people due to manufacturer's negligence all because a snail got into a bottle of ginger beer. Or did it?

The article I wrote questioned whether there ever had been a snail or a bottle. The court case was a matter of law and no decomposing snail or bottle was part of the evidence. In my view, it was an opening up of a new market for lawyers. Two interesting responses to my article came after publication. Firstly, I received an email from a lawyer in Vancouver, Canada asking whether the language, thoughts, ideas and expressions in my piece were completely original. I emailed one word: 'Absolutely!' and never heard from him again. I had no idea what he was on about but I read somewhere that a law professor in Canada claims to have the original bottle - a claim that I am very sceptical about. Stevenson was a large manufacturer of aerated waters and sold thousands of bottles of ginger beer every week. However, the case did give rise to a Glasgow expression: 'Gees a slug o' your ginger!'

I sent the finished article to the *Scots Magazine* who agreed to publish it in their 2009 August edition. I had been trying to get something published for years, and all of a sudden, I had two published articles published within three months of each other and was paid for both. This encouraged me to continue with my writing and I started working on a second novel, *The Italian Connection*.

Around the middle of the year I also became involved with an Australian group who planned to transport the clipper ship, *City of Adelaide*, to Australia. The HMS *Carrick*, as she was previously known, was a three-masted clipper ship that had been berthed at the Broomielaw in Glasgow since 1949. At that time the ship served as a Royal Navy Voluntary Reserve club, but in 1990 it was sold to the Clyde Ship Trust for the nominal fee of one pound. Eventually, it was towed to Irvine where it lay grounded for years. Prior to its Royal Navy Service, the clipper had spent many years sailing to Australia with migrants seeking a new life. It is estimated that a quarter of a million South Australians can trace their origins to passengers who emigrated to South Australia on the ship.

Mr. Genders, my old boss in Farquharson Brothers, was a former Royal Navy Captain and a member of the committee who ran the club. I was sent to deliver a message to him at the ship and I was allowed aboard. I remember it had chandeliers hanging from the black painted ceilings, the seating was circular with plush red upholstery and the tables covered with brilliant white cloth and silver cups and decanters. The flooring was a highly polished wood and in beautiful condition with portholes embedded in the white walls.

In 2009 I wrote on a website that I'd been aboard the ship, as I now stayed in Irvine. I later received an email from a member of the Australian group who were negotiating the acquisition of the ship with a view to taking her back to Adelaide. Over the next few months, I photographed and videoed the ship and harbour entrance and sent the results to Peter Roberts, a naval architect involved in the negotiations. When he came to Scotland, I was invited to meet him and it was interesting to hear how they proposed to move the vessel from Irvine to Australia. However, there was another competing group interested in taking the ship to Sunderland, where it was built. One former Sunderland councillor, who named his daughter Adelaide after the ship, climbed aboard and occupied it for a few days but nobody paid him much attention apart from the local paper who gave him and his protest a mention. The MP for the area wrote in the local newspaper that it would be impossible to get the ship to Australia given its condition, but the Aussies were made of sterner stuff.

A large crowd watched as the *City of Adelaide* was loaded aboard a barge in Irvine harbour and towed out to sea. The ship now sits in Adelaide harbour. It is my understanding that they do not intend to restore the ship but to preserve her.

Chapter Eighteen

An Idea for a Novel

I had an idea, and a file full of notes, for a novel that involved reincarnation, spiritualism, a catholic priest, a World War II soldier and a serial killer. The character of the soldier, and his early life in London, was to be based on the writings of a colleague's father who had begun to write his autobiography but sadly passed on before he finished it. My colleague, Ann Giles, passed me her dad's incomplete manuscript that I had agreed to edit where I could. George Giles seemed the ideal person on which to base the character of the soldier and those parts of the book that feature George are factual. The rest is fictional. The Giles family very kindly allowed me to use some of their dad's work for which I was, and still am, very grateful. I wanted to write a story that moved quite fast, like one of my favourite novels, *The 39 Steps*. I wanted a book that kept the reader guessing, a book free from gratuitous sex and violence, and a book with a controversial end. After two or three years of research and writing I thought I had just about achieved that end, when *The Italian Connection* was finished.

However, it was not easy to decide a genre into which the book would easily sit, which made placing it with a publisher quite difficult. It is not a crime novel, although there are a number of crimes committed in the course of the story. It is not a science fiction story, but there are elements of that genre within the writings, nor can it be accurately described as a courtroom drama, although a court case is a core part of the tale. If it has to be described at all it is perhaps best to call it a mystery novel.

George Giles, the main character, tries to come to terms with the fact that he has been propelled fifty-five years into the future. Readers encounter, and are presented with, ideas about spiritualism, mediumship, life-after-death, reincarnation and psychiatric and psychological theories involving dual or multiple-personality disorders. These themes are linked with a serial killer and courtroom drama with a twist in the end. A fellow author wrote that the book is 'a beguiling tale, which challenges normal assumptions about time, place and identity, as well as being an adventure story of high quality.' One reader wrote on Amazon that it was 'a story which gets you thinking on many different levels. Well thought out, well written and keeps you interested right to the end.' I hope the latter is true for those who read it.

I sent the manuscript off to a few publishers one of whom wrote back saying they felt it was a good story but were rejecting it on the grounds that it was too short. I had never read anything so ridiculous, and wrote a sharp email telling these misguided people that my novel was longer than *The Communist Party Manifesto*, - a book that changed the world. Longer than Steinbeck's *Of Mice and Men*, longer than Buchan's *The 39 Steps*, and longer than hundreds of other books. Eventually I found a Scottish publisher who was accepting submissions from Scottish authors and I thought I would have another go. I sent the manuscript with a covering letter and awaited yet another rejection slip. But it never came. What came was an invitation to meet with Sandy Jamieson, a Director of Ringwood Publishing based in Glasgow.

We met in the tearoom at the Botanic Gardens, and Sandy asked me a number of questions about the book and my own background. I outlined my writing experience and some of my almost forty full-time jobs, and added that to keep myself busy, I represented friends and acquaintances who had issues with faulty goods, the DWP, trouble at work and other problems.

I was quite encouraged by what Sandy was saying about the book and absolutely delighted when he said Ringwood were interested in publishing it. He warned me that it was difficult for most writers to make money from the process, but I was simply happy that a real publisher was willing to take the book on, and that I was about to become a published author. He told me that he was considering publication in May the following year. I remember saying I could be dead by then to which came the classic response: 'Posthumous authors sell better.' He went on to say a contract would follow and that almost ruined my becoming a published author, due to my screw-up with an email.

I had received an email from Sandy after our meeting that said the contract would arrive 'the first week...' But it didn't say the first week of what. I intended to forward it to my pal Janice, and added a note saying: 'Contract due first week of ...' what? Lent? The new fitba'season? Pregnancy? and I said I was irritated. Unfortunately, I clicked on 'reply all' and sent it straight back to Sandy, who replied as follows:

'I typed "next week" or so I thought, but obviously my typing skills are as bad as your email-sending skills. My initial reaction to your irritation was to suggest that to save your wick any further stress we might make it the first week of never, to allow you more time to find a bigger, more efficient publisher. On further reflection, I remember the need to distinguish between authors and books, and the need to recognise that irritation comes from many sources, and imperfections on both sides is part of that. So, I apologise for my typing error and will send a contract to you to arrive no later than the 21st of November.'

My big mouth almost lost me the publication but I defined his remark, about distinguishing between authors and their books, as meaning the author may be a numpty but the book is okay.

As to his comment that posthumous authors sell better, I had forgotten to tell him I was already dead according to the Bank of Scotland and a Manchester debt collector.

It began in August 2008 when a letter addressed to 'The Estate of Mr John Keeman' arrived at my home. It offered condolences on my death and outlined a sum of money owing at the time of the '...unfortunate passing of Mr John Keeman.' It claimed that the sender was acting on behalf of Halifax Bank of Scotland and enclosed a leaflet on Probate. The latter was absolutely useless as presumably I had died in Scotland, and the English Probate process has no place in Scots Law. I raised a complaint with both the bank and the debt collector. The bank replied some weeks later saying they were still investigating and the debt collector sent another letter again referring to the estate of the late John Keeman. My son Stephen called them and asked them to stop referring to his father as being dead, as it was upsetting his mother, and I was due to go to hospital for heart surgery. They assured him they would but when I phoned them five hours later, they asked if I was calling about the estate of the late John Keeman. 'I am John Keeman, you fucking half-wit!' I roared down the phone.

I raised a complaint about HBOS with the Banking Ombudsman but frankly they were as much use as a one-armed wallpaper hanger. I then enlisted the help of a financial journalist from the *Daily Record* who wrote to the bank and the debt collector saying she was going to run a piece on my untimely death and asking for comment. The debt collector apologised and said they wished to settle the claim but refused to comment further or provide a name. However, they rang her back later with a different approach and a statement that read:

'We are very pleased to discover Mr John Keeman is alive and well...as specialists in handling such sensitive communications, we conduct ourselves with the utmost care and compassion...'

The journalist emailed me asking if I wished to comment on their statement and I replied: 'This quote is sometimes attributed to Abraham Lincoln or Mark Twain, but I believe it to be by an Irish author of many years ago who said: 'It is sometimes better to keep your mouth shut and appear a fool, than to open it and remove any doubt.'

Following some email correspondence, the debt-collector agreed to pay me five-hundred pounds and a further two-hundred direct to the British Heart Foundation. I waited three weeks before I phoned the Foundation and, as I suspected, they had not received any money. I wrote a stern email to the debt-collectors and threatened court action within three weeks; a few days later on 20th March 2009, I got a thank-you letter from BHF. However, that did not end the matter.

In 2014, around the time I was discussing publication of *The Italian Connection*, I was receiving similar letters from the same debt-collector again addressed to the Estate of the late John Keeman. Almost five years later they had not amended their records. I again took the matter up with the Banking Ombudsman but again they were pretty useless. I discovered that the Manchester debt-collectors were owned by an American company and I threatened to sue them through their Head Office in the United States. That gave them a push and they apologised and wrote-off everything I owed to HBOS, who were as useless as the Ombudsman in handling my complaints. If I'm honest I secretly wish they would start sending similar letters again. I could use a few bob.

Sandy was as good as his word and I was assigned an editor, Keira, whom I met in Waterstones on Sauchiehall Street. She was a lovely girl, but had the irritating habit of putting milk in Earl Grey tea. Despite this, her assistance was greatly appreciated and she contributed to my changing the ending which I believe improved my original. I was happy to recognise her contributions in the published version.

In May 2015 my book was launched in a pub at Charing Cross. The event was quite well attended and I was very surprised when the real George Giles' daughter, Ann, came over to my table and asked me to sign her book. I recognised her voice immediately and almost dropped my pen with shock. Ann was a lovely person and was my supervisor for a while before I was promoted. She was as honest as the day is long and I remember when she became a manager the company organised a training weekend that involved some competitive events and staying in a camp in Perth. Two Land Rovers were hired and one allocated to each team. Ann told me that the vehicles had arrived and were parked in our underground car park so I went down to have a look. As I suspected the keys were left inside both vehicles so I called upstairs and asked Ann if she knew which one was hers. She told me and I removed the keys from the other one. I went upstairs and had a chat with her. When I suggested that, as points were being awarded for the team who found their way to the camp first, she should put them in a drawer somewhere in the office. Then after her team had a thirty- or forty-minutes head start she should phone in and tell them where they were. She was absolutely mortified with the idea and insisted she would never do such a thing and it was totally unfair. My view was it was using initiative which was part of the training course, apparently. In the event both teams drove off at around the same time. I never did find out who got to Perth first.

As to the book launch, the night went very well with my pals Janice and Ray from the BBC coming along. Ray and Janice's partner agreed to do readings I selected. Ray was reading part of a speech by the Irish priest and I specifically asked him not to use an Irish accent. Of course, he ignored me, as any pal would. An old college friend also turned up, along with lots of people I did not know. It would be lovely to say that the book hit a bestsellers list but despite our best efforts it didn't.

I had a lengthy piece written by an *Evening Times* journalist but that seemed to concentrate more on my former jobs than the book and in a way encouraged the writing of this autobiography. I also did an interview with local radio in Irvine but there was no significant response. From my part I was happy to have the novel published, but of course publishers are in the business of selling books. I created a website and I later recorded a YouTube interview with another of Ringwood's editorial staff. Perhaps Sandy is right and when I'm gone a Hollywood producer will turn up with an offer for the film rights.

Following the publication of my two articles by the *Scots Magazine* I had submitted a third which they rejected, saying that whilst the main character was born in Scotland his adventures on the high seas took place elsewhere. The article was about a Skelmorlie-born man, William Watson, whose escapades during the American Civil war, as a blockade runner, formed the character Rhett Butler in Margaret Mitchell's best-selling novel and blockbuster film: *Gone with the Wind.*

Watson left Skelmorlie as a young man and headed for the Bahamas where he worked as an engineer in the cotton and sugar mills. A few years later, looking to form his own business, he moved to the town of Baton Rouge, Louisiana. By 1860, Watson had become a well-respected member of the local business community. He was a member of the local militia and when the American Civil War began, he volunteered along with other 'fine spirited young fellows,' and became a confederate soldier in the Baton Rouge Pelican Rifles.

In June 1862 his time as a volunteer was over and he was discharged at Tupelo, Mississippi. When he returned to

Baton Rouge as a civilian, his business premises and other buildings in which he had a financial interest had been razed to the ground. He sold off his remaining assets and invested in a sailing ship called the Rob Roy and eventually ran the blockade. His plan was to outrun the Yankee Navy with a load of cotton which would fetch a high price in Havana. In the Gulf of Mexico, the ship was fired upon by a Yankee gun boat and a cannon ball damaged much of the uninsured cargo but she made port and discharged her goods. Five months after the Rob Roy had sailed into Texas waters, she was ready to run to sea with a load of cotton worth thirty-thousand dollars - about three quarters of a million dollars in today's terms. After outrunning Yankee ships, she arrived in Tampico, Mexico, where she discharged part of her load and set sail for Havana. In the Cuban capital, Watson sold off his share of the cotton, and negotiated for a cargo consisting of two-hundred Enfield rifles with bayonets, four-hundred Belgian muskets also with bayonets, four-hundred cavalry swords, twenty-five boxes of ammunition, six cases of saddlery equipment, currycombs, horse brushes, bales of blankets, clothing, boots, and some luxury items like tea, cheese and spices. Shipping alcohol into the Confederacy was forbidden unless it was for medical purposes, but in Watson's experience the arrival of a blockade runner often produced an outbreak of sickness among the local customs officers and administrators, so he took on a measure of alcohol as well.

Watson continued quite a successful career as a blockade runner before returning to Scotland at the end of the war. He built three villas in his home village of Skelmorlie, two of which, Pea Ridge and Oakhill, he named after civil-war battles. In retirement Watson wrote two books at his Pea Ridge villa, one about his time in the Confederate Army and the other about his adventures as a blockade runner. It was the latter book that led Margaret Mitchell to fashion the character Rhett Butler.

In 2017 I received a call from STV presenter Angus Simpson. The former ITV news reader was now presenting STV's *Peoples History Show*, and he told me he'd read my piece on William Watson and STV wanted to do a four-minute film for the programme. I said I was happy for them to use whatever parts of the article they wanted but he said he wanted me to take part in telling the story. I agreed, and a few days later Angus arrived with a colleague and we set off for Largs cemetery where we filmed at Watson's graveside. From there we went to Skelmorlie and received permission to film in and around Watson's 'Beechgrove' villa. The villa has an enormous garden that stretches downhill almost to the main Largs Road. It provides a wonderful view across the Clyde and in his retirement, Watson must have sat and gazed toward the Atlantic that carried him on his adventures all those years ago. It was a very interesting day and I looked forward to seeing the finished piece. Frankly I was a little sceptical that the story could be cut to four minutes, but I didn't figure on the editing and photographic skills of Dr Marco Federici. The broadcast went out on the 16th of October 2017.

Chapter Nineteen

Another Visit to Hospital

One problem with writing an autobiography is deciding when to stop, unless of course you drop dead sometime during the process. Lord Cockburn's autobiographical diary is an example of the latter. The former Scottish High Court Judge wrote every night about his days in court, his travel arrangements when he was on circuit, the friends he stayed with, where he had lunch, the weather and other personal interests. Someone else made the last entry by writing that the Judge had passed away peacefully in his sleep. I suppose I should finish my writings now that I am in my seventy-seventh year and unlikely to achieve much else worth writing about. It is March 2020 as I write this chapter.

Last year I awoke in hospital with no idea why I was there. The last thing I could recall was having difficulty walking, so I was cautious about getting out of bed. There were signs I'd had a drip inserted but it was no longer there and I decided to get up. My walking stick was lying against a chair, so I reached out, picked it up and tried to stand. I did so without difficulty and took a few tentative steps but my balance was fine. I strolled up and down a corridor with no ill effects and decided to lie down on the bed until someone appeared to tell me what was going on. Pretty soon a nurse appeared with a tray holding a pot of tea, milk and sugar and a croissant and butter. Heaven! I tucked in and after I'd finished, a doctor appeared. He stood a good bit away from the end of the bed, stretched out his arms and began to wiggle his fingers. 'What am I doing?' he asked.

'Standing there looking ridiculous,' I replied.

'What day is it?' was his second question.

'Thursday,' I said with a great deal of confidence.

'Now who's being ridiculous?' he said. 'It's eight-thirty on Friday morning. You were brought in on Wednesday night with a very high temperature and fever but things have settled down. We'll see how you are over the next few hours and if everything remains stable you can go home.'

He left without further comment along with his entourage of nurses. I called home and spoke with Janet who told me that when she came home around nine on the Wednesday evening, I was in bed running a temperature and gibbering, more than usual. She called an ambulance and I was taken to hospital but released around half-past two in the morning, when Stephen drove me home. According to Janet, I was still as bad in the morning so another ambulance was called and I was taken back to hospital. Now, on Friday morning, I was fully aware of my environment but had lost a full two days. I still cannot remember being taken to hospital or anything that happened until I woke up in hospital on the Friday morning. About two weeks later I received a letter asking me to attend hospital for an X-ray. It was during this procedure that the radiologist said I'd had a bout of pneumonia. Fortunately, the scan showed it had cleared up. I'd been taken to hospital twice by ambulance but still have no recollection of either trip. However, I remember very clearly being in an ambulance on May 20th 2018 and being treated for a head injury.

It was a Sunday and I drove down to the beach for a walk along the sands and some ozone. At the mouth of the river, I noticed a small ship had holed on the rocks and I went down the rocky hill to take some pictures. Suddenly I slipped, went up in the air and fell backwards with my head striking the rocks. I was winded and could not breathe properly. I genuinely thought I was a goner, and lay there on

231

my back trying to recover my breath. A man came down to where I was lying and told me his wife had gone for help. Slowly, I began to recover my breath and put my hand to my head feeling what could only be blood. Within minutes two staff from Irvine Coast Watch appeared and got me into a sitting position, wrapped me up in what looked like an enormous roll of tinfoil and a blanket. They told me to remain seated until the ambulance arrived. When it did, one of the crew cleaned my head wound and closed it up with a glue-like substance. The other had me linked up to monitors, measuring my heart rate, blood pressure, temperature and asked me some questions about medication, my general health and so on. I told him I was feeling much better and figured I'd be okay. He assumed I was retired and asked me what I did to pass the time. I said I did some rock climbing but obviously I wasn't very good at it, and that I also wrote a bit. He asked the standard question when someone mentions that they write:

'Have you had anything published?'

I think my answer surprised him a bit when I said I'd had a novel published and one or two other things. I told him the title of my book and a little bit about the story. Within a couple of minutes, he'd bought a copy on-line. I was okay to go home after treatment and a friend drove my son Stephen down to the beach to pick up our car and drive me home. I did not feel well enough to drive myself. I mentioned to the publishers on Facebook later that day that the ambulance driver had bought a copy of the book and a couple of the Ringwood authors very sympathetically wrote:

'That's a hell of a way to try and sell a book, John,' and 'Great idea John. I'm just about to throw myself down the stairs.'

Funny guys!

I had the opportunity to look back to the past at the beginning of August 2018 when I went to Loch Fad. My visit was to see Donald Campbell's restored speedboat: 'Bluebird.' Campbell was killed when attempting to break the world water speed record when Bluebird crashed on Coniston Water on the Lake District, on the 4th of January 1967.

I parked the car in Wemyss Bay station and got the ferry across to the Isle of Bute. When I disembarked, I hired a taxi to take me out to the loch but the driver said he could only take me to the start of a farm road and I'd have to walk from there. I asked him how far it was and he said about half a mile. After tramping over a narrow pathway strewn with rocks and mud pools for about forty minutes, I spotted a farmhouse sitting on a bend off the track near the loch side.

'It can't be far now,' I said to myself when suddenly the high-pitched whine of a jet engine shattered the peaceful countryside. As I rounded the bend, I saw a crowd of people with the Bluebird parked on a slipway at the side of the loch. The taxi driver obviously had no concept of distance but it was well worth the walk to see this icon of British engineering and ingenuity.

I was only twenty-three when I saw the crash on the television. Speed is something most young men enjoy, and I was no different. And of course, as a truck driver, speeding fines went with the territory. It was quite a sight to see the speedboat restored to her former glory sitting proudly on a Scottish loch. One guy I spoke with had come from Melbourne to see it, but I was not looking forward to my walk back to civilisation. When I finally got home that evening, I fell asleep in my chair. I expect after these experiences I've written about it is probably time to slow down a bit, cut back on the travelling and stop clambering over rocks. Maybe I should buy a Billy Connolly big slipper and cozy up to the fire. I certainly won't be writing anything as lengthy as a novel again but I expect I'll still write the odd letter to the newspapers complaining about companies who inject water into my bacon and complain about politicians on Facebook.

We'll see! As my best friend Janice would say it's only another few months to Christmas.

It was Janice that I was on my way to visit one Friday in March 2019, when I fell foul of traffic cameras on the south side of Glasgow. I received three pictures from Glasgow City Council showing my Renault Megane driving in a bus lane. There is not a bus in any of the pictures. This idea of discriminating on behalf of buses is just another car-tax racket like parking charges.

Chapter Twenty

The End of the Road

The Bible tells us that 'there is a time to be born and a time to die.' I am glad I was born when I was, despite the horrific housing conditions, diseases and poverty. When I compare what today's young people have to go through in terms of getting work and a place to live I know they have it a lot harder than I ever did. I truly do not believe I could get through the exigencies of today's society without ending up in prison for assaulting some government lackey.

In my younger days, I could turn up at the local labour exchange, or Buroo, as it was known colloquially, and select what sort of job I wanted to do. Workers were in control of their own destiny. No little fascist sitting behind a desk could force me into applying for any old job. I'd have laughed at the idea of a target set by the government saying I had to apply for a certain number of jobs every day or lose benefit. But things have changed and in my view for the worse. In our present society government spokespersons and economists talk about the 'job market.' It is not a job market, it's a slave market! At the centre of this so-called market lie zero-hour contracts. The use of the term contract is misleading *per se*. In law the parties to a contract are supposed to be at arms-length with each other; but that is pure nonsense in terms of a zero hours contract. In these arrangements all the power lies with the employer. They should be named 'slave arrangements.' A couple of years ago some companies began employing people without paying them anything at all. Among these cowboys was a well-known pound shop franchise. When challenged on this offer of unpaid jobs, their glib response was to say the people gained experience and doing the work enhanced their self-esteem. Glasgow comedian Kevin Bridges had a routine in which he said that their self-esteem was less than enhanced when they were working in a shop where everything was worth a pound - apart from them.

No matter what schemes these companies come up with they can always find some bullshit artist who glibly tries to defend the practice, no matter how obnoxious it may be. One of the worst examples of this twisted logic occurred many years ago in the so-called Land of the Free. It is an old case but attitudes like that of the judge still flourish among many present-day politicians who are capable of twisting the law to get the result they want, usually to the advantage of their business friends. In the Adkins case, the District of Columbia state legislators, concerned about the number of poorly-paid women who were turning to prostitution, passed a minimum-wage law. This was challenged by companies in the Supreme Court on the grounds that the right to a minimum wage was an 'unconstitutional infringement of their right to freely negotiate a contract.' It took a further fourteen years before the same court overturned this twisted decision. Be careful when you hear any politician or businessman in the UK lobbying for a written constitution - it's not worth the paper it would be written on. At least the lack of a written constitution gives a system some flexibility. The Adkins case held back equal-pay laws for around fourteen years. Another decision by the Supreme Court that proposed the doctrine of 'Separate but Equal,' was not unconstitutional, but allowed racism to flourish for sixty years, before it was repealed by more enlightened thinkers.

Some evidence presented by the Office for National Statistics a couple of years ago revealed that women and young people are most affected by these slave arrangements. Nearly two-thirds of those on zero-hours are women, and a third are in the 16 to 24-year-old age group. They are offered by some of the largest companies in the world, and although many MPs have condemned them over the years, they do nothing about making them unlawful. It is unlikely with the UK being out of Europe that they will. In fact, many people argue that worker's rights will be reduced when we finally leave the European Union. There is absolutely no security for people on zero-hour contracts. They cannot plan things like social events, holidays, treats for children, paying bills and other normal activities. This leads many of them into poor mental health. But if you believe that the Government gives a toss, then look at how they have been treating the sick and disabled. I have been involved in a number of cases over the years assisting colleagues, family, friends and acquaintances with appeals against the denial of basic benefits or rights at work. It is no coincidence that the Government changed the name of the Department of Health and Social Security to the Department of Work and Pensions. When the government start changing the names of their departments it is not change for changes sake. When I was young, we had a Minister for War; now it is the Minister for Defence. Subtle, eh?

The change of name by the DSS to the DWP signalled the demise of social security for many people, in particular the disabled. Almost half a million people have lost benefits with the switch from Disability Living Allowance to Personal Independence Payments. It should be noted that these claimants were already declared as disabled by medical professionals and it beggars belief that our family doctors were ever that naïve that they couldn't spot a malingerer. Today, private companies are paid by the taxpayer to reduce the amount of benefits paid to disabled and sick people. The medical professionals they use are mostly barely-qualified nurses or paramedics. If you study some of the decisions it becomes clear that they take a template approach to marking application forms. Around the country terms like 'the applicant was well kempt,' frequently appear in decisions by the DWP. It is an arcane term and it is extremely unlikely that the young nurses and paramedics who are carrying out these assessments would know what it meant if you asked them. It is straight out of some civil service manual of terms to annoy people with.

The latest appeal I handled was decided in January 2020. The claimant had been diagnosed with Parkinson's Disease, but at her assessment she was awarded zero points. The process if you are refused a benefit requires you to ask for a 'mandatory reconsideration.' This is just a time-wasting tactic employed by the DWP to discourage people from continuing with their claim. Currently people have to wait around ten weeks or more to get a decision. What claimants have to do is write back to the DWP to ask the officer who awarded them no points to change the decision. In the majority of cases it never happens. It is only when a claimant has gone through this farce that the right to appeal to an Independent Tribunal comes into play. However, unlike other civil courts, the DWP do not have to appear, and a claimant cannot cross-examine the individual who made the decision that left them having to seek assistance from the food banks (so much applauded by one particularly irritating Member of Parliament, Jacob Rees-Mogg). Murderers and rapists have the right to cross-examine their accusers, but not a disabled social security claimant. They're having a laugh.

Under the threat of an appeal, in the case I mentioned, the DWP backed down and re-assessed their decision. This time they awarded the Parkinson's sufferer twenty-four points. I cannot believe that within a few weeks of upholding their original decision of zero points, they found twenty-four points in the claimant's favour rather than allow the tribunal to go ahead with the appeal. I was not surprised by result. The decision of awarding zero points was riddled with 'lies, damned lies and statistics,' as well as illogical conclusions.

My considered opinion is that the DWP reconsidered their original decision to avoid themselves embarrassment at an Appeal Tribunal and more exposure of the fact that barely qualified former nurses and paramedics are making decisions on claimants with very complex diseases.

In light of my experience in dealing with employment rights and current benefits legislation I believe if I was a young man today, I would struggle to cope. I would either be in jail or perhaps driven to suicide like so many of our current young people. With the lack of real jobs to apply for and the pressure they are put under to find work that is just not available; it is not surprising that many of them lose hope and end it all. The UK is one of the richest countries in the world but that wealth is in the hands of the few. Meanwhile there are people sleeping in the streets, and little by way of government action to alleviate the problem.

A former Tory MP was claimed to have described the homeless as: 'people you step over when you come out of the opera.' Maybe we can expect that from a Tory, but a Labour MP took to Twitter a couple of years ago writing that he spotted four beggars near the entrance to one of his watering holes, saying they should have been moved on.

I do not believe our welfare state is safe in the hands of people like this or people like Ian Duncan Smith who was awarded a knighthood for putting the sick and disabled into poverty. The following is an extract from the letter I sent my MP it relates to the two cases I was dealing with at the time:

'... those who have their benefit stopped can ask for the decision to be reviewed. This can take up to ten weeks and during the whole of that time the benefit is withdrawn. If the decision stands, which it does in most cases, because you are writing to the same person and asking them to change their mind - this is the equivalent of asking a jury, that has just found you guilty, to change their mind. When the decision is held to stand you can then apply for an independent appeal which can take over three months before it's heard. All of this time no benefit is being paid. If you are a convicted murderer in this country you can be restored to your original position pending an appeal immediately it is lodged but not if you are an unemployed sick, poor or disabled person.'

It is a sad day in any society when murderers and rapists have more rights than the disabled. Over a quarter of a million disabled people have had their benefits removed or refused under this wholly discredited system. It appears that the Tory ethos is the old arcane view that the disabled are being punished by God for their sins. I would bet my hard-earned pension, that millionaires like Rees-Mogg, who is proud of foodbanks, and Duncan-Smith, who spends the equivalent of half a week's unemployment benefit on a breakfast, subscribe to such views. The Tories have also removed the term Social Security from the benefits regime which speaks volumes for their attitude toward our unemployed, poor sick and disabled citizens, and the welfare state in general.

The test of any nation is how well or badly it treats these citizens. I regret we are falling lower and lower down the ladder. I cannot remember a time when the poor and disabled were under such an attack by their own government. I think we have to go back to the days of the 'poor's house' to find such ill treatment. Moreover, these companies who carry out these assessments are luring newly-qualified nurses and paramedics from the NHS, giving them little training and encouraging them to fail as many assessments as they can. In effect these poorly-qualified assessors are overruling or ignoring advice about a patient's health given by GPs, psychiatrists, psychologists and other highly qualified medical professionals. The evidence for this is that almost two-thirds of PIP Assessments have been overturned by the Independent Appeal Services. What kind of government tolerates paying companies millions of pounds of taxpayer's cash, when the recipients of that cash get almost three-quarters of their decisions wrong. This by itself is a national disgrace and an incompetence of government at the highest level but can we expect less from those who, by and large, are recipients of inherited wealth who have never done a hard day's work in their lives.

My hope is that before long our young people can have the same opportunities I had to work and to achieve a high standard of education without having to put themselves into debt to do so.

Article 8 of the European Convention on Human Rights protects your right to respect for your private life, your family life, your home and your correspondence. But the right to respect for your home does not give you a right to housing. This is the sort of bullshit we ought to be doing something about. A job and somewhere decent to live should be at the heart of any law that claims to be concerned with human rights. I lived in squalor for a while when I was young but at least a single end could be made warm and provided shelter from the elements. I expect that nothing much will change no matter how much I rant about present day politicians and businesses. I suppose while we have two pensioners in their nineties living in a building with over six-hundred rooms and access to dozens more properties, nothing is likely to change. Perhaps someday people who live on benefits will have a representative body with the power to act on their behalf to ensure they are treated with dignity and respect and not as spongers. But they will have to organise it themselves and will get no assistance from politicians to whom the welfare state is anathema. At the time of writing our whole economic and welfare systems are under attack. Not from Tory politicians but from a virus. On the evidence presented so far things will be very different when it is over. Maybe our superiors will learn something about the strength of a united people but that is probably wishful thinking.

Just before the last general election I wrote to my

MP a fifteen-hundred-page letter complaining about PIP assessments. The Scottish Parliament will soon take responsibility for some social security benefits, including PIP. If they continue to use private companies who employ nurses to assess people with complex medical problems, including mental health issues, it is unlikely the system will change much. We need to get back to dealing with how the illness affects the sufferer rather than PIP that only concerns itself with whether someone can cook themselves a meal or walk a particular distance. Along with Universal Credit, these benefits represent the archaic thinking that there are poor and a deserving poor and being disabled is a punishment for one's sins. There is no place in a modern welfare state for people who believe such tripe!

I know I have fewer years in front of me than behind. It has been a long life but I would not say a happy one. I've never understood what happiness means anyway. Sometimes I've felt content with my lot and on other occasions depressed about it. I've felt great joy at the birth of my sons and great sadness at the loss of James. It is said a parent should not bury a child but in reality, it happens every day and each loss is a tragedy for those left behind. I have loved and been loved, met many lovely people and some real bastards, so I suppose there's been balance in my life. I have many memories to look back on when I'm older and I still love reading, music, sailing on the Firth of Clyde and sitting on the beach watching the ocean darken as the sun goes down.

The End

About the Author

John Keeman was born during the Second World War in Anderston, into a harsh environment of poor housing, ill-health and poverty. He grew up alongside the development of a healthier, more cooperative, society where slum clearance policies, the creation of the National Health Service, the development of a Social Security safety net and a strong Trade Union movement ameliorated the worst conditions and provided a degree of collective support.

John's life was still in the main a hard struggle to keep steady employment and to provide adequately for his family. He became a fighter for justice for his fellow men and women, always pushing against the system.

Now retired, he writes and has had several short stories and one novel, the *Italian Connection* published by Ringwood.

Acknowledgements

It is difficult, if not impossible, to write a book without the assistance of other people and it is fair and reasonable that such help should be recognized. My sincere thanks to Ringwood Publishing staff; Sandy Jamieson, who encouraged me to write about my life, Isobel Freeman and Kevin McGowan who shared the unenviable task of editing and proof reading, Mia Atwooll for her contribution to the back cover, Olivia Simpson who designed the book's website, Nicola Campbell who designed the cover and Ruth McQueeney who wrote a welcome introductory piece on the publisher's website.

I would also like to thank school teacher Janice Burrows, a dear friend who has supported my writing for many years.

Finally my wife and sons for their tolerance.

Some other books from Ringwood Publishing

The Italian Connection

John Keeman

In George Giles' mind, he is a twenty-seven year old soldier preparing to return home after Germany's surrender during World War II. But his body tells a different story; he is the serial killer Peter Hunter. Unlike Hunter, George has never killed, nor does he know of the 21st Century.

Faced with a London much changed from his memories, George seeks answers from the past and tries to uncover how he is connected to Hunter.

ISBN: 978-1-901514-20-9   £9.99

Ronnie – A Dog-Owner's Guide to Fulfillment

Susan Campbell

Ronnie tells the heart-warming story about how a dog, the power of positive thought and perseverance can completely change your life for the better. Ronnie, a rescue dog from the Dogs Trust, changes the life of husband and wife Susan and Colin Campbell for ever. Showing that a dog is never simply a pet.

ISBN: 978-1-901514-29-2   £9.99

Memoirs of a Feminist Mother

Carol Fox

As a committed feminist, Carol Fox has achieved success for very many women, but her greatest battle described in this book was very personal. Following serious fertility problems, Carol made the positive decision to become a single parent by choice, to have a child while she still could. Refused access to fertility treatment in Scotland she had no choice but to move to London. Through sheer determination and tenacity, Carol obtained treatment in England in the early 1990s and her daughter was born in 1992, following extensive fertility treatment and battles against judgemental attitudes which appear almost vindictive to us 25 years later. Her story has attracted media coverage, sparking debates on motherhood and the right to be a single parent in the UK.

ISBN: 978-1-901514-21-6   £9.99

Memoirs of Franz Schreiber

Charles P. Sharkey

The Memoirs of Franz Schreiber gives a unique perspective on the trials and turmoil of life in Germany between the wars. When Franz Schreiber and his mother get the news that his beloved father would not be returning to their home in Berlin from the battle fields of the First World War, their lives changed in unimaginable ways. Following Franz as he grows into a man, the effects of war are endless, and the story of his life is littered with love, tragedy and danger.

ISBN: 978-1-901514-64-3   £9.99

Not the Life Imagined

Anne Pettigrew

A darkly humorous, thought-provoking story of Scottish medical students in the sixties, a time of changing social and sexual mores.

Beth Slater is shocked at how few female medical students there are and that some people, think they shouldn't be there at all. Devastated by a close friend's suicide, Beth uncovers a revealing diary and vows to find the person responsible for her death.

Beth charts the students' changing, often stormy, relationships over two decade. In time, indiscretions surface with dire consequences for some.

ISBN: 978-1-901514-70-4   £9.99

Jinx Dogs Burns Now Flu

Alex Gordon

Alex Gordon spills the beans in a frank and candid manner!

Jinx Dogs Burns Now Flu is a rollicking, hilarious trip through the crazy world of Scottish newspapers. It's a journey that takes the reader behind the headlines of the biggest, most sensational stories of our national press.

Some stories here throw an entirely new light on what actually happened around many of Scotland's most famous sports stars; stories that will cause quite a few reputations to be reassessed!

ISBN: 978-1-901514-28-5   £9.99

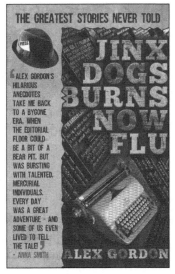